TEST PREPARATION

DSST®

Personal Finance Exam Secrets Study Guide

DEAR FUTURE EXAM SUCCESS STORY

First of all, **THANK YOU** for purchasing Mometrix study materials!

Second, congratulations! You are one of the few determined test-takers who are committed to doing whatever it takes to excel on your exam. **You have come to the right place.** We developed these study materials with one goal in mind: to deliver you the information you need in a format that's concise and easy to use.

In addition to optimizing your guide for the content of the test, we've outlined our recommended steps for breaking down the preparation process into small, attainable goals so you can make sure you stay on track.

We've also analyzed the entire test-taking process, identifying the most common pitfalls and showing how you can overcome them and be ready for any curveball the test throws you.

Standardized testing is one of the biggest obstacles on your road to success, which only increases the importance of doing well in the high-pressure, high-stakes environment of test day. Your results on this test could have a significant impact on your future, and this guide provides the information and practical advice to help you achieve your full potential on test day.

Your success is our success

We would love to hear from you! If you would like to share the story of your exam success or if you have any questions or comments in regard to our products, please contact us at **800-673-8175** or **support@mometrix.com**.

Thanks again for your business and we wish you continued success!

Sincerely,
The Mometrix Test Preparation Team

Need more help? Check out our flashcards at:
http://MometrixFlashcards.com/DSST

Written and edited by the Mometrix Exam Secrets Test Prep Team
Printed in the United States of America

Table of Contents

Introduction

Thank you for purchasing this resource! You have made the choice to prepare yourself for a test that could have a huge impact on your future, and this guide is designed to help you be fully ready for test day. Obviously, it's important to have a solid understanding of the test material, but you also need to be prepared for the unique environment and stressors of the test, so that you can perform to the best of your abilities.

For this purpose, the first section that appears in this guide is the **Secret Keys**. We've devoted countless hours to meticulously researching what works and what doesn't, and we've boiled down our findings to the five most impactful steps you can take to improve your performance on the test. We start at the beginning with study planning and move through the preparation process, all the way to the testing strategies that will help you get the most out of what you know when you're finally sitting in front of the test.

We recommend that you start preparing for your test as far in advance as possible. However, if you've bought this guide as a last-minute study resource and only have a few days before your test, we recommend that you skip over the first two Secret Keys since they address a long-term study plan.

If you struggle with **test anxiety**, we strongly encourage you to check out our recommendations for how you can overcome it. Test anxiety is a formidable foe, but it can be beaten, and we want to make sure you have the tools you need to defeat it.

Secret Key #1 – Plan Big, Study Small

There's a lot riding on your performance. If you want to ace this test, you're going to need to keep your skills sharp and the material fresh in your mind. You need a plan that lets you review everything you need to know while still fitting in your schedule. We'll break this strategy down into three categories.

Information Organization

Start with the information you already have: the official test outline. From this, you can make a complete list of all the concepts you need to cover before the test. Organize these concepts into groups that can be studied together, and create a list of any related vocabulary you need to learn so you can brush up on any difficult terms. You'll want to keep this vocabulary list handy once you actually start studying since you may need to add to it along the way.

Time Management

Once you have your set of study concepts, decide how to spread them out over the time you have left before the test. Break your study plan into small, clear goals so you have a manageable task for each day and know exactly what you're doing. Then just focus on one small step at a time. When you manage your time this way, you don't need to spend hours at a time studying. Studying a small block of content for a short period each day helps you retain information better and avoid stressing over how much you have left to do. You can relax knowing that you have a plan to cover everything in time. In order for this strategy to be effective though, you have to start studying early and stick to your schedule. Avoid the exhaustion and futility that comes from last-minute cramming!

Study Environment

The environment you study in has a big impact on your learning. Studying in a coffee shop, while probably more enjoyable, is not likely to be as fruitful as studying in a quiet room. It's important to keep distractions to a minimum. You're only planning to study for a short block of time, so make the most of it. Don't pause to check your phone or get up to find a snack. It's also important to **avoid multitasking**. Research has consistently shown that multitasking will make your studying dramatically less effective. Your study area should also be comfortable and well-lit so you don't have the distraction of straining your eyes or sitting on an uncomfortable chair.

The time of day you study is also important. You want to be rested and alert. Don't wait until just before bedtime. Study when you'll be most likely to comprehend and remember. Even better, if you know what time of day your test will be, set that time aside for study. That way your brain will be used to working on that subject at that specific time and you'll have a better chance of recalling information.

Finally, it can be helpful to team up with others who are studying for the same test. Your actual studying should be done in as isolated an environment as possible, but the work of organizing the information and setting up the study plan can be divided up. In between study sessions, you can discuss with your teammates the concepts that you're all studying and quiz each other on the details. Just be sure that your teammates are as serious about the test as you are. If you find that your study time is being replaced with social time, you might need to find a new team.

Secret Key #2 – Make Your Studying Count

You're devoting a lot of time and effort to preparing for this test, so you want to be absolutely certain it will pay off. This means doing more than just reading the content and hoping you can remember it on test day. It's important to make every minute of study count. There are two main areas you can focus on to make your studying count.

Retention

It doesn't matter how much time you study if you can't remember the material. You need to make sure you are retaining the concepts. To check your retention of the information you're learning, try recalling it at later times with minimal prompting. Try carrying around flashcards and glance at one or two from time to time or ask a friend who's also studying for the test to quiz you.

To enhance your retention, look for ways to put the information into practice so that you can apply it rather than simply recalling it. If you're using the information in practical ways, it will be much easier to remember. Similarly, it helps to solidify a concept in your mind if you're not only reading it to yourself but also explaining it to someone else. Ask a friend to let you teach them about a concept you're a little shaky on (or speak aloud to an imaginary audience if necessary). As you try to summarize, define, give examples, and answer your friend's questions, you'll understand the concepts better and they will stay with you longer. Finally, step back for a big picture view and ask yourself how each piece of information fits with the whole subject. When you link the different concepts together and see them working together as a whole, it's easier to remember the individual components.

Finally, practice showing your work on any multi-step problems, even if you're just studying. Writing out each step you take to solve a problem will help solidify the process in your mind, and you'll be more likely to remember it during the test.

Modality

Modality simply refers to the means or method by which you study. Choosing a study modality that fits your own individual learning style is crucial. No two people learn best in exactly the same way, so it's important to know your strengths and use them to your advantage.

For example, if you learn best by visualization, focus on visualizing a concept in your mind and draw an image or a diagram. Try color-coding your notes, illustrating them, or creating symbols that will trigger your mind to recall a learned concept. If you learn best by hearing or discussing information, find a study partner who learns the same way or read aloud to yourself. Think about how to put the information in your own words. Imagine that you are giving a lecture on the topic and record yourself so you can listen to it later.

For any learning style, flashcards can be helpful. Organize the information so you can take advantage of spare moments to review. Underline key words or phrases. Use different colors for different categories. Mnemonic devices (such as creating a short list in which every item starts with the same letter) can also help with retention. Find what works best for you and use it to store the information in your mind most effectively and easily.

Secret Key #3 – Practice the Right Way

Your success on test day depends not only on how many hours you put into preparing, but also on whether you prepared the right way. It's good to check along the way to see if your studying is paying off. One of the most effective ways to do this is by taking practice tests to evaluate your progress. Practice tests are useful because they show exactly where you need to improve. Every time you take a practice test, pay special attention to these three groups of questions:

- The questions you got wrong
- The questions you had to guess on, even if you guessed right
- The questions you found difficult or slow to work through

This will show you exactly what your weak areas are, and where you need to devote more study time. Ask yourself why each of these questions gave you trouble. Was it because you didn't understand the material? Was it because you didn't remember the vocabulary? Do you need more repetitions on this type of question to build speed and confidence? Dig into those questions and figure out how you can strengthen your weak areas as you go back to review the material.

Additionally, many practice tests have a section explaining the answer choices. It can be tempting to read the explanation and think that you now have a good understanding of the concept. However, an explanation likely only covers part of the question's broader context. Even if the explanation makes perfect sense, **go back and investigate** every concept related to the question until you're positive you have a thorough understanding.

As you go along, keep in mind that the practice test is just that: practice. Memorizing these questions and answers will not be very helpful on the actual test because it is unlikely to have any of the same exact questions. If you only know the right answers to the sample questions, you won't be prepared for the real thing. **Study the concepts** until you understand them fully, and then you'll be able to answer any question that shows up on the test.

It's important to wait on the practice tests until you're ready. If you take a test on your first day of study, you may be overwhelmed by the amount of material covered and how much you need to learn. Work up to it gradually.

On test day, you'll need to be prepared for answering questions, managing your time, and using the test-taking strategies you've learned. It's a lot to balance, like a mental marathon that will have a big impact on your future. Like training for a marathon, you'll need to start slowly and work your way up. When test day arrives, you'll be ready.

Start with the strategies you've read in the first two Secret Keys—plan your course and study in the way that works best for you. If you have time, consider using multiple study resources to get different approaches to the same concepts. It can be helpful to see difficult concepts from more than one angle. Then find a good source for practice tests. Many times, the test website will suggest potential study resources or provide sample tests.

Practice Test Strategy

If you're able to find at least three practice tests, we recommend this strategy:

Untimed and Open-Book Practice

Take the first test with no time constraints and with your notes and study guide handy. Take your time and focus on applying the strategies you've learned.

Timed and Open-Book Practice

Take the second practice test open-book as well, but set a timer and practice pacing yourself to finish in time.

Timed and Closed-Book Practice

Take any other practice tests as if it were test day. Set a timer and put away your study materials. Sit at a table or desk in a quiet room, imagine yourself at the testing center, and answer questions as quickly and accurately as possible.

Keep repeating timed and closed-book tests on a regular basis until you run out of practice tests or it's time for the actual test. Your mind will be ready for the schedule and stress of test day, and you'll be able to focus on recalling the material you've learned.

Secret Key #4 – Pace Yourself

Once you're fully prepared for the material on the test, your biggest challenge on test day will be managing your time. Just knowing that the clock is ticking can make you panic even if you have plenty of time left. Work on pacing yourself so you can build confidence against the time constraints of the exam. Pacing is a difficult skill to master, especially in a high-pressure environment, so **practice is vital**.

Set time expectations for your pace based on how much time is available. For example, if a section has 60 questions and the time limit is 30 minutes, you know you have to average 30 seconds or less per question in order to answer them all. Although 30 seconds is the hard limit, set 25 seconds per question as your goal, so you reserve extra time to spend on harder questions. When you budget extra time for the harder questions, you no longer have any reason to stress when those questions take longer to answer.

Don't let this time expectation distract you from working through the test at a calm, steady pace, but keep it in mind so you don't spend too much time on any one question. Recognize that taking extra time on one question you don't understand may keep you from answering two that you do understand later in the test. If your time limit for a question is up and you're still not sure of the answer, mark it and move on, and come back to it later if the time and the test format allow. If the testing format doesn't allow you to return to earlier questions, just make an educated guess; then put it out of your mind and move on.

On the easier questions, be careful not to rush. It may seem wise to hurry through them so you have more time for the challenging ones, but it's not worth missing one if you know the concept and just didn't take the time to read the question fully. Work efficiently but make sure you understand the question and have looked at all of the answer choices, since more than one may seem right at first.

Even if you're paying attention to the time, you may find yourself a little behind at some point. You should speed up to get back on track, but do so wisely. Don't panic; just take a few seconds less on each question until you're caught up. Don't guess without thinking, but do look through the answer choices and eliminate any you know are wrong. If you can get down to two choices, it is often worthwhile to guess from those. Once you've chosen an answer, move on and don't dwell on any that you skipped or had to hurry through. If a question was taking too long, chances are it was one of the harder ones, so you weren't as likely to get it right anyway.

On the other hand, if you find yourself getting ahead of schedule, it may be beneficial to slow down a little. The more quickly you work, the more likely you are to make a careless mistake that will affect your score. You've budgeted time for each question, so don't be afraid to spend that time. Practice an efficient but careful pace to get the most out of the time you have.

Secret Key #5 – Have a Plan for Guessing

When you're taking the test, you may find yourself stuck on a question. Some of the answer choices seem better than others, but you don't see the one answer choice that is obviously correct. What do you do?

The scenario described above is very common, yet most test takers have not effectively prepared for it. Developing and practicing a plan for guessing may be one of the single most effective uses of your time as you get ready for the exam.

In developing your plan for guessing, there are three questions to address:

- When should you start the guessing process?
- How should you narrow down the choices?
- Which answer should you choose?

When to Start the Guessing Process

Unless your plan for guessing is to select C every time (which, despite its merits, is not what we recommend), you need to leave yourself enough time to apply your answer elimination strategies. Since you have a limited amount of time for each question, that means that if you're going to give yourself the best shot at guessing correctly, you have to decide quickly whether or not you will guess.

Of course, the best-case scenario is that you don't have to guess at all, so first, see if you can answer the question based on your knowledge of the subject and basic reasoning skills. Focus on the key words in the question and try to jog your memory of related topics. Give yourself a chance to bring the knowledge to mind, but once you realize that you don't have (or you can't access) the knowledge you need to answer the question, it's time to start the guessing process.

It's almost always better to start the guessing process too early than too late. It only takes a few seconds to remember something and answer the question from knowledge. Carefully eliminating wrong answer choices takes longer. Plus, going through the process of eliminating answer choices can actually help jog your memory.

Summary: Start the guessing process as soon as you decide that you can't answer the question based on your knowledge.

How to Narrow Down the Choices

The next chapter in this book (**Test-Taking Strategies**) includes a wide range of strategies for how to approach questions and how to look for answer choices to eliminate. You will definitely want to read those carefully, practice them, and figure out which ones work best for you. Here though, we're going to address a mindset rather than a particular strategy.

Your odds of guessing an answer correctly depend on how many options you are choosing from.

Number of options left	5	4	3	2	1
Odds of guessing correctly	20%	25%	33%	50%	100%

You can see from this chart just how valuable it is to be able to eliminate incorrect answers and make an educated guess, but there are two things that many test takers do that cause them to miss out on the benefits of guessing:

- Accidentally eliminating the correct answer
- Selecting an answer based on an impression

We'll look at the first one here, and the second one in the next section.

To avoid accidentally eliminating the correct answer, we recommend a thought exercise called **the $5 challenge**. In this challenge, you only eliminate an answer choice from contention if you are willing to bet $5 on it being wrong. Why $5? Five dollars is a small but not insignificant amount of money. It's an amount you could afford to lose but wouldn't want to throw away. And while losing $5 once might not hurt too much, doing it twenty times will set you back $100. In the same way, each small decision you make—eliminating a choice here, guessing on a question there—won't by itself impact your score very much, but when you put them all together, they can make a big difference. By holding each answer choice elimination decision to a higher standard, you can reduce the risk of accidentally eliminating the correct answer.

The $5 challenge can also be applied in a positive sense: If you are willing to bet $5 that an answer choice *is* correct, go ahead and mark it as correct.

Summary: Only eliminate an answer choice if you are willing to bet $5 that it is wrong.

Which Answer to Choose

You're taking the test. You've run into a hard question and decided you'll have to guess. You've eliminated all the answer choices you're willing to bet $5 on. Now you have to pick an answer. Why do we even need to talk about this? Why can't you just pick whichever one you feel like when the time comes?

The answer to these questions is that if you don't come into the test with a plan, you'll rely on your impression to select an answer choice, and if you do that, you risk falling into a trap. The test writers know that everyone who takes their test will be guessing on some of the questions, so they intentionally write wrong answer choices to seem plausible. You still have to pick an answer though, and if the wrong answer choices are designed to look right, how can you ever be sure that you're not falling for their trap? The best solution we've found to this dilemma is to take the decision out of your hands entirely. Here is the process we recommend:

Once you've eliminated any choices that you are confident (willing to bet $5) are wrong, select the first remaining choice as your answer.

Whether you choose to select the first remaining choice, the second, or the last, the important thing is that you use some preselected standard. Using this approach guarantees that you will not be enticed into selecting an answer choice that looks right, because you are not basing your decision on how the answer choices look.

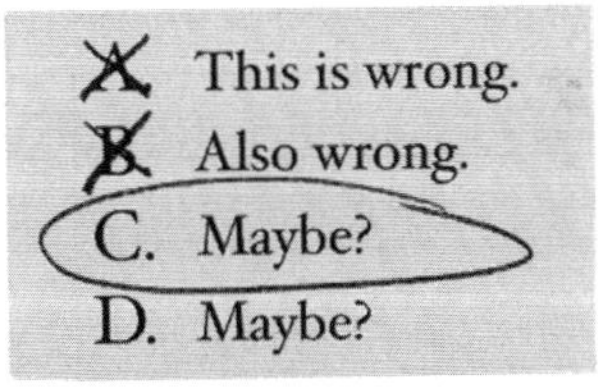

This is not meant to make you question your knowledge. Instead, it is to help you recognize the difference between your knowledge and your impressions. There's a huge difference between thinking an answer is right because of what you know, and thinking an answer is right because it looks or sounds like it should be right.

Summary: To ensure that your selection is appropriately random, make a predetermined selection from among all answer choices you have not eliminated.

Test-Taking Strategies

This section contains a list of test-taking strategies that you may find helpful as you work through the test. By taking what you know and applying logical thought, you can maximize your chances of answering any question correctly!

It is very important to realize that every question is different and every person is different: no single strategy will work on every question, and no single strategy will work for every person. That's why we've included all of them here, so you can try them out and determine which ones work best for different types of questions and which ones work best for you.

Question Strategies

✓ Read Carefully

Read the question and the answer choices carefully. Don't miss the question because you misread the terms. You have plenty of time to read each question thoroughly and make sure you understand what is being asked. Yet a happy medium must be attained, so don't waste too much time. You must read carefully and efficiently.

✓ Contextual Clues

Look for contextual clues. If the question includes a word you are not familiar with, look at the immediate context for some indication of what the word might mean. Contextual clues can often give you all the information you need to decipher the meaning of an unfamiliar word. Even if you can't determine the meaning, you may be able to narrow down the possibilities enough to make a solid guess at the answer to the question.

✓ Prefixes

If you're having trouble with a word in the question or answer choices, try dissecting it. Take advantage of every clue that the word might include. Prefixes can be a huge help. Usually, they allow you to determine a basic meaning. *Pre-* means before, *post-* means after, *pro-* is positive, *de-* is negative. From prefixes, you can get an idea of the general meaning of the word and try to put it into context.

✓ Hedge Words

Watch out for critical hedge words, such as *likely, may, can, often, almost, mostly, usually, generally, rarely,* and *sometimes.* Question writers insert these hedge phrases to cover every possibility. Often an answer choice will be wrong simply because it leaves no room for exception. Be on guard for answer choices that have definitive words such as *exactly* and *always.*

✓ Switchback Words

Stay alert for *switchbacks.* These are the words and phrases frequently used to alert you to shifts in thought. The most common switchback words are *but, although,* and *however.* Others include *nevertheless, on the other hand, even though, while, in spite of, despite,* and *regardless of.* Switchback words are important to catch because they can change the direction of the question or an answer choice.

☑ FACE VALUE

When in doubt, use common sense. Accept the situation in the problem at face value. Don't read too much into it. These problems will not require you to make wild assumptions. If you have to go beyond creativity and warp time or space in order to have an answer choice fit the question, then you should move on and consider the other answer choices. These are normal problems rooted in reality. The applicable relationship or explanation may not be readily apparent, but it is there for you to figure out. Use your common sense to interpret anything that isn't clear.

Answer Choice Strategies

☑ ANSWER SELECTION

The most thorough way to pick an answer choice is to identify and eliminate wrong answers until only one is left, then confirm it is the correct answer. Sometimes an answer choice may immediately seem right, but be careful. The test writers will usually put more than one reasonable answer choice on each question, so take a second to read all of them and make sure that the other choices are not equally obvious. As long as you have time left, it is better to read every answer choice than to pick the first one that looks right without checking the others.

☑ ANSWER CHOICE FAMILIES

An answer choice family consists of two (in rare cases, three) answer choices that are very similar in construction and cannot all be true at the same time. If you see two answer choices that are direct opposites or parallels, one of them is usually the correct answer. For instance, if one answer choice says that quantity *x* increases and another either says that quantity *x* decreases (opposite) or says that quantity *y* increases (parallel), then those answer choices would fall into the same family. An answer choice that doesn't match the construction of the answer choice family is more likely to be incorrect. Most questions will not have answer choice families, but when they do appear, you should be prepared to recognize them.

☑ ELIMINATE ANSWERS

Eliminate answer choices as soon as you realize they are wrong, but make sure you consider all possibilities. If you are eliminating answer choices and realize that the last one you are left with is also wrong, don't panic. Start over and consider each choice again. There may be something you missed the first time that you will realize on the second pass.

☑ AVOID FACT TRAPS

Don't be distracted by an answer choice that is factually true but doesn't answer the question. You are looking for the choice that answers the question. Stay focused on what the question is asking for so you don't accidentally pick an answer that is true but incorrect. Always go back to the question and make sure the answer choice you've selected actually answers the question and is not merely a true statement.

☑ EXTREME STATEMENTS

In general, you should avoid answers that put forth extreme actions as standard practice or proclaim controversial ideas as established fact. An answer choice that states the "process should be used in certain situations, if..." is much more likely to be correct than one that states the "process should be discontinued completely." The first is a calm rational statement and doesn't even make a definitive, uncompromising stance, using a hedge word *if* to provide wiggle room, whereas the second choice is far more extreme.

☑ Benchmark

As you read through the answer choices and you come across one that seems to answer the question well, mentally select that answer choice. This is not your final answer, but it's the one that will help you evaluate the other answer choices. The one that you selected is your benchmark or standard for judging each of the other answer choices. Every other answer choice must be compared to your benchmark. That choice is correct until proven otherwise by another answer choice beating it. If you find a better answer, then that one becomes your new benchmark. Once you've decided that no other choice answers the question as well as your benchmark, you have your final answer.

☑ Predict the Answer

Before you even start looking at the answer choices, it is often best to try to predict the answer. When you come up with the answer on your own, it is easier to avoid distractions and traps because you will know exactly what to look for. The right answer choice is unlikely to be word-for-word what you came up with, but it should be a close match. Even if you are confident that you have the right answer, you should still take the time to read each option before moving on.

General Strategies

☑ Tough Questions

If you are stumped on a problem or it appears too hard or too difficult, don't waste time. Move on! Remember though, if you can quickly check for obviously incorrect answer choices, your chances of guessing correctly are greatly improved. Before you completely give up, at least try to knock out a couple of possible answers. Eliminate what you can and then guess at the remaining answer choices before moving on.

☑ Check Your Work

Since you will probably not know every term listed and the answer to every question, it is important that you get credit for the ones that you do know. Don't miss any questions through careless mistakes. If at all possible, try to take a second to look back over your answer selection and make sure you've selected the correct answer choice and haven't made a costly careless mistake (such as marking an answer choice that you didn't mean to mark). This quick double check should more than pay for itself in caught mistakes for the time it costs.

☑ Pace Yourself

It's easy to be overwhelmed when you're looking at a page full of questions; your mind is confused and full of random thoughts, and the clock is ticking down faster than you would like. Calm down and maintain the pace that you have set for yourself. Especially as you get down to the last few minutes of the test, don't let the small numbers on the clock make you panic. As long as you are on track by monitoring your pace, you are guaranteed to have time for each question.

☑ Don't Rush

It is very easy to make errors when you are in a hurry. Maintaining a fast pace in answering questions is pointless if it makes you miss questions that you would have gotten right otherwise. Test writers like to include distracting information and wrong answers that seem right. Taking a little extra time to avoid careless mistakes can make all the difference in your test score. Find a pace that allows you to be confident in the answers that you select.

⊘ Keep Moving

Panicking will not help you pass the test, so do your best to stay calm and keep moving. Taking deep breaths and going through the answer elimination steps you practiced can help to break through a stress barrier and keep your pace.

Final Notes

The combination of a solid foundation of content knowledge and the confidence that comes from practicing your plan for applying that knowledge is the key to maximizing your performance on test day. As your foundation of content knowledge is built up and strengthened, you'll find that the strategies included in this chapter become more and more effective in helping you quickly sift through the distractions and traps of the test to isolate the correct answer.

Now that you're preparing to move forward into the test content chapters of this book, be sure to keep your goal in mind. As you read, think about how you will be able to apply this information on the test. If you've already seen sample questions for the test and you have an idea of the question format and style, try to come up with questions of your own that you can answer based on what you're reading. This will give you valuable practice applying your knowledge in the same ways you can expect to on test day.

Good luck and good studying!

Foundations

FINANCIAL PLANNING PROCESS

The financial planning process involves setting personal financial goals and devising plans and strategies to meet those goals. It is important to first figure out what your financial goals are. Then, create and implement strategies that will help you reach your goals. Put budgets into place that track progress toward your goals and see that they are being met. Check financial statements regularly to see that you're planning and budgeting are working, and make adjustments where necessary. If your financial situation changes, amend goals and strategies as needed.

TERM FINANCIAL GOALS

Financial goals are based upon future possessions or activities a person wants to obtain. These things can include large purchases (e.g., home, car, boat) or things such as college, a vacation, or retirement. It is important to assign specific monetary values to these things so that financial goals can be set and specific plans can be made to achieve them. To get in good financial shape, it is important to:

- Create, maintain, and update financial records that are organized, accurate, and complete
- Develop a budget that will work for you and that you can stick to
- Reward yourself now and then with minor extravagances to help you stay motivated in regards to larger financial goals
- Put together a retirement savings plan and start contributing to it
- Prepare for unexpected/ unforeseen circumstances by establishing an emergency savings account

RETIREMENT FINANCIAL PLANNING ASSUMPTIONS

There are a number of assumptions people have in terms of financial planning for retirement that are not accurate. One is that retiring at age sixty is a reasonable goal. Due to medical advancements, people are living much longer; this means they will then need more money to retire on than previous generations. Another assumption is that it is possible to retire comfortably on 75 percent of preretirement income. In fact, people need almost 100 percent of their preretirement income to retire comfortably, due to the increase in healthcare costs. Many people also assume that pension and Social Security will cover at least half of their living expenses; however, since neither of these sources are as stable as in the past, it is likely retirees will need 401(k) or other retirement savings to help cover living expenses.

PSYCHOLOGY OF MONEY

The psychology of money is found in the way people view money, its level of importance in their lifestyles, and their financial goals. These decisions are guided by individual value systems and motivations. The need to satisfy basic needs such as food, shelter, and clothing is a primary motivator for most people. Someone motivated by ego, status, and power may be driven to acquire wealth in order to obtain status symbols such as expensive homes, cars, clothes, toys, and exotic vacations. Someone who values family or less stress in life may choose money-making venues that are less risky and time-consuming, but also less potentially financially rewarding.

PERSONAL FINANCIAL STATEMENTS

Personal financial statements help track financial progress. They provide a current financial update indicative of your overall financial state, indicate possible sources of future financial challenges, and guide you toward sound financial decisions. Reviewing financial statements helps you set reachable goals, work toward them, and assess how you are progressing.

There are two types of personal financial statements: the balance sheet and the income and expense statement. A balance sheet shows net worth at a particular point in time by subtracting debts owed from assets. This provides a good indication of overall financial position. An income and expense statement shows financial performance over time, and is helpful for comparing set budgets to the actual expenses that were incurred. It is important to look carefully at this statement in order to correct any negative financial results in the future.

Cash Budget

A cash budget takes into account expected cash receipts and expenses, such as savings and investments, for the upcoming year. Reviewing income and expenses each month is useful. A cash budget is prepared by estimating income and expenses. Keep in mind that changes in lifestyle or cost of living will impact a cash budget, so include them when estimating income and expenses.

Annual Budget in the Red

If your annual budget is still negative after you've reduced expenses, there are still some things you can do. Increase income by getting a higher-paying job or part-time work on the side. Liquidating savings and investments to make up for a budget shortfall is another option; however, this contradicts the reason for budgeting, which is setting realistic financial goals that you can meet both in the present and future. The third option is to review the budget and eliminate the least essential expenses. This option does not require dipping into savings or making adjustments in other areas.

Budget Control Schedule

A budget control schedule is a brief overview showing how actual income and expenses sync with your budget and where there are discrepancies. When looking at these discrepancies, try to figure out why they happened and what you can do to prevent them from happening again. By examining this schedule each month, it's easier to spot where income is coming up short and makes adjustments. Only the most extreme circumstances should require you to finance budget adjustments with borrowing money, or using savings and investments.

Estimating Income and Expenses

In order to determine your income for the next year, include take-home pay, bonuses and commissions, pension or annuity income, and investment income. Take a look at financial records from past years to help you project expenses for the coming year, and keep in mind your short-term financial goals. If you have not kept good financial records, old checkbook registers and credit card statements can also help you estimate expenses. If you do not have any past financial records to go on, you can estimate what you expect your future expenses to be and assign dollar values to those anticipated expenses.

Cash Management and Liquid Assets

Cash management is the way cash and near-cash resources are managed and used. Liquid assets are also called near-cash resources since they're held in cash and do not lose value as non-liquid assets can when they are converted to cash. Checking and savings accounts, money market deposit accounts, money market mutual funds, CDs, and other short-term investment vehicles are also considered liquid assets. It is important to have successful cash management so that there is enough money for both current living expenses and future savings.

Personal Property and Real Property

Personal property is property than can easily be moved, such as jewelry, cars, clothing, electronics, furniture, and appliances. Personal property usually decreases in value with use. Real property is a physical asset that cannot be moved such as land or buildings. Real property generally has a long life span and a dollar value that increases over time. Fair market value is what an asset is actually worth, meaning the dollar amount it could command in the marketplace.

Personal Balance Sheet

A personal balance sheet should be prepared at least annually and more frequently if possible. First, list the current market value for all assets. To get an accurate number for liquid and investment assets, look at checking, savings, and investment account statements.

The Kelley Blue Book will help determine the value of your car, and by checking advertisements for comparable homes you can get an idea of the value of yours. Second, write down short-term and long-term liabilities, and be sure to include charges that may not have shown up on your statement yet. Third, calculate your net worth. Subtract the total of all of your liabilities from the total of all of your assets and this will give you the equity of your total assets.

Income and Expense Statement

An income and expense statement shows where and how money is being spent. There are three parts to it: income, expenses, and cash surplus (the difference between your income and expenses).

The income and expense statement is done on a cash basis, which means it only uses those transactions that involve actual cash receipts. A balance sheet only shows one's financial situation at a given point in time, whereas an income and expense statement shows all of the financial activities that occurred over a period of time.

Preparing an Income and Expense Statement

A good income and expense statement will give you a bottom line for your cash flow. Start by writing down all income sources for a select time period. You can gather this through bank and investment statements, paycheck stubs, tax refunds, and the sales of any assets. Then, put together expense categories that make sense for your particular needs, such as housing, utilities, food, transportation, medical, clothing, insurance, taxes, personal care, recreation/entertainment, and appliances/furniture, etc. Be sure to include any other categories that apply specifically to you. Then, subtract total expenses from total income to determine whether you have a cash surplus or deficit.

Financial Record Keeping

It is important to keeping accurate, up-to-date, and organized financial records in order to prepare accurate personal financial statements and budgets, pay less for tax preparation, make sure to receive all tax deductions to which you are entitled, pay less in taxes, and make it easier for someone else to handle your finances should something happen to you.

It is a good idea to track financial statements when you create your budget each year and record the information in a ledger. Getting a safe deposit box for essential or sensitive documents is important. Prepare an inventory of everything you own and owe. Use an expandable file with compartments for bills, receipts, and paycheck stubs, but keep separate files for tax planning records.

How long to keep financial records

There are some good rules of thumb for where and how long to keep financial records. ATM and deposit slips can be destroyed as soon as the transactions show up on the bank statement. Short-term papers (six months or less) can be filed to be readily available. Once you receive year-end statements for bank, mutual funds, 401(k) s, and paycheck stubs, you can shred the monthly statements; keep year-end statements for three years.

Keep tax returns, instruction manuals, records of home capital improvements and the like for seven years. All permanent papers, such as birth certificates, passports, wills, and insurance policies, should be kept in a bank safe-deposit box. Keep current photos, height and weight measurements, fingerprints of your children and medical records for the whole family readily accessible in case you need them quickly in an emergency.

Economy's major players

The three major players in the economy are government, business, and consumers. The government is divided into three levels: federal, state, and local governments. Each of these levels provides goods and services including defense, public schools, police and fire protection, roads and bridges. Businesses allow for a free enterprise system in which the choices consumers make determines the goods and services businesses will provide. The spending habits of consumers directly impact the economy. When consumers spend more, the economy is strong; when consumers spend less, the economy is weaker.

Four economic cycle stages

The upward and downward shift of economic activity creates an economic cycle which typically has four stages: expansion, recession, depression, and recovery. During the expansion phase, levels of employment and production are high and the economy is booming with an increase in the price of goods and services. A recession occurs when economic expansion has peaked and then declines for six months. When a recession continues to decline until the economy slows drastically, a depression occurs. During the recovery phase, employment and production begin to again increase. Gross domestic product (GDP) takes into account all of the goods and services produced in a particular time frame in order to monitor economic growth.

Inflation

When prices increase over time, inflation is the cause. Inflation is crucial to financial planning because it affects income and what consumers pay for goods and services. Low rates of inflation create a thriving economy.

CPI

The consumer price index (CPI) is a way to measure inflation based on how much the costs of goods and services change.

Purchasing power

Purchasing power is how much a dollar will buy at any point in time.

Financial Modernization Act of 1999

The Financial Modernization Act of 1999, also known as the Gramm-Leach-Biley Act or GLB Act, has provisions that protect personal financial information entrusted to financial institutions. The Financial Privacy Rule, the Safeguards Rule, and pretexting provisions control how information can be gathered and shared.

The Financial Privacy Rule controls how a company collects personal information and how it can be disclosed. Customers are provided with a written privacy notice that clearly describes how private information might be used. The Safeguards Rule mandates the responsibility of financial institutions to develop and maintain protections to shield customer information. Pretexting provisions protect customers from an unauthorized party obtaining their personal financial information under false pretenses.

Financial Institutions Classification

Financial institutions can be classified as non-depository or depository.

- Nondepository financial institutions do not accept deposits but do perform services similar to those offered by banks, including issuing credit cards and allowing a limited number of checks to be written. Nondepository financial institutions include stock brokerage firms, mutual funds, and life and finance companies.
- Most financial transactions occur at depository financial institutions which include savings banks, credit unions, S&Ls, and commercial banks. Since their services and products are similar, depository financial institutions are usually referred to as banks even though different agencies regulate them. What sets these institutions apart is that they accept deposits, allowing people use them frequently for their checking and savings accounts

Time Value of Money

A dollar is worth more now than it will be at a certain point in the future; this is the definition of time value of money. Dollar values can be accurately compared at different points in time. If you earn interest on investments (excluding taxes and other unforeseen factors) you should want to receive equal amounts of money sooner rather than later. If you know what your financial goals are as well as what your expected savings or investment earning are, you should be able to calculate how much to save or invest each year.

Future Value of Money

Future value of money is how much a specific amount of money will be worth, given a specific interest rate over a given period of time. The growth in value occurs from both earned interest and compounding interest. Compounding happens when the yearly interest earned is left in the account and becomes part of the balance (principal) on which interest is earned in following years.

Future value can be used to calculate the growth of an investment over time, or to determine how much must be saved to accumulate a certain amount of money by a specified date in the future. Both approaches can be used to determine long-term financial goals monetary values.

Future Value of a Single Amount vs. Future Value of an Annuity

To calculate the future value for a single amount of money, multiply the amount invested by the future value factor (the value that an amount today will grow to if it earns a specific amount of interest over a certain time period).

An annuity is a fixed amount of money. To figure the future value of an annuity, take that amount and divide it by the future value annuity factor (this corresponds to a given year and an interest rate).

Present Value of Money

Present value of money is how much money needs to be invested now at a certain interest rate over a specified period of time in order to reach a desired future amount. In order to determine the present value, you need to apply discounting. Discounting the future value at the interest rate the money could earn over a specified time period provides the present value of an amount of money you can get at a point in the future. Discounting is the opposite of compounding, and used to determine the future value of money.

Credit and Debt

LIABILITIES

A liability is a debt that has to be repaid. Installment loans, credit card charges, mortgages on housing or other real estate result in liabilities. There are two types of liabilities, short-term (current) and long-term.

Short-term liability refers to a debt that requires repayment within a year of the date on the balance sheet. Short-term liabilities include taxes, medical bills, insurance premiums, utilities, and rent.

Long-term liabilities refer to debt that needs to be paid one year or more from the date of the balance sheet. A good example of a long-term liability is a student loan or real estate mortgage.

IMPORTANCE OF CREDIT

Credit allows individuals and companies to purchase goods and services when sufficient cash is not available. It allows businesses, governments, and consumers to make transactions and supply the goods and services consumers demand. Credit allows businesses and governments to employ people and provide various projects and programs; these boost the economy and raise our standards of living. Consumer credit permits the purchase of expensive items without jeopardizing the budge; however, the buy now, pay later mentality can lead to serious financial problems, including bankruptcy.

CREDIT USE

People use credit in order to buy things that cost more than they can currently afford. One reason people use credit is because it is convenient. Credit cards are accepted almost everywhere and are quicker and easier than writing a check. The second reason people use credit is to make large purchases, such as homes and cars, without having to use cash. Sometimes people borrow part of the purchase amount and repay it on a loan schedule basis. This way, people can receive an expensive asset immediately and make small payments over time. Credit also provides a way to cover a financial emergency in unforeseen situations like illness or employment. Credit can also be used to partially fund finance investment options.

ESTABLISHING CREDIT

Opening a checking and savings account will show lenders that you are financially responsible and will help you establish credit. Opening one or two credit card accounts and using them now and then (being careful not to overdo it) will also prove that you are a reliable credit customer. Even if you do not need a loan, getting a small one (and putting it in a CD or money market account) can help establish a good credit history.

Any interest that accumulates can be used to cover the expense on the loan, especially if you pay it off ahead of schedule. Do not pay off the loan too quickly since lenders are looking for evidence of financial responsibility over a period of time. You may want a larger loan in the future, and your ability to get this will be based in part on your past history of paying off small loans.

CREDIT DANGER SIGNS

There are a number of credit card danger signs to watch out for. Taking sixty to ninety days to pay bills that used to be paid in thirty; struggling to make minimum payments; or ignoring bills altogether out of fear are signs of credit danger. Using a credit card for impulse purchases, exceeding borrowing limits, and using cards to pay off other debts are clear warning signs.

You should also be concerned if you have no savings, are using more than 20 percent of your take-home pay to pay credit card bills and personal loans, are postdating checks to keep them from bouncing, or borrowing money for simple day-to-day standard living expenses. Finally, it should serve as a red flag if collection agencies repeatedly call.

Strong Credit History

You can build a strong credit history and maintain credit-worthiness in a number of ways. When first applying for credit, be honest; credit agencies will do a thorough background check and misinformation will only hurt your credibility. Avoid overextending yourself and only use credit when you can afford the repayment schedule. Make sure that you live up to all of the terms of the credit card and be on time with monthly payments. If you will not be able to make a payment, let the lender know; often they will work with you.

Women's Credit Problems

Lenders once viewed women as credit risks because they could become pregnant and lose their jobs. The Equal Credit Opportunity Act (ECOA) removed creditors' ability to consider marital status or child-bearing plans, and mandated lenders must consider a woman's income on the same basis as the man's. Divorced and widowed women may not have an established credit history, making it difficult for them to get credit. This can be avoided by using one's own name when filling out credit card applications, reporting any information to the credit bureau using the maiden name, and keeping a separate credit file.

Line of Credit

Line of credit is the most credit a customer can have at any given time as determined by the issuer of the credit card. An applicant can request a certain amount, and this is taken into consideration along with the applicant's financial status.

Cash Advance

A cash advance is a loan that banks or other financial institutions offer a credit card holder. The advance happens at a bank but the transactions are like merchandise purchases. Instead of receiving a good or service, the person receives a check or cash.

Base Rate

When giving loans to individuals and small/medium size business, the rate of interest banks use is called the base rate.

5 Cs of Credit

The 5 Cs of Credit are the five things a lender looks at when trying to determine how well a borrower will be able to repay a loan.

- Character is demonstrated by how well a borrower lives up to the loan's requirements
- Capital refers to the borrower's assets
- Collateral secures the loan and can be claimed by the lender in the event of default
- Capacity is whether the borrower will pay back the loan in a timely manner
- Condition looks outside the individual borrower's profile to any economic factors that could affect whether the borrower can pay back the loan

Open Account Credit

Open account credit is a type of credit given to a consumer before any transaction takes place and is often offered by either a retail store/merchant or financial institution. Retail stores and merchants give consumers open account credit in order to promote their products and often offer special incentives or benefits for using them. Financial institutions provide general-purpose credit cards and overdraft protection lines as well as secured and unsecured revolving lines of credit. These are often banks but can also include S&Ls, credit unions, major stock-brokerage firms, and consumer finance companies.

Credit Limit

Credit limit is the dollar amount set by the offering credit institution that the consumer is specified that not allowed to go over when borrowing.

Credit Statement

A credit statement is a summary of all of the transactions, payments, interest charges, and fees that occurred in a recent time period (usually a month).

Bank Credit Cards Fees

There are several kinds of bank credit card fees, one of which is the annual fee. This is an annual charge for the use of a credit card, although it may be waived the first year and possibly after that if you ask.

A transaction fee occurs each time there is a cash advance, and a late payment fee is charged when you are late making a payment. When balances are transferred between cards, a balance transfer fee if usually assessed.

When traveling overseas, be aware of any foreign transaction fees or currency conversion fees.

If you go over your credit limit, you may be charged an over-the-limit fee.

Finally, if you do not use your credit card for a long time, you may be charged a non-usage fee.

Debit Card

A debit card is used for cash transactions; it is different from a credit card because there are no finance charges to pay and the money is not a loan but a withdrawal of existing funds. Debit cards offer the convenience of credit cards without their interest rates.

They do not offer a line of credit; they can be overdrawn unless they are used with care. Also, there can be a $50-500 charge if a debit card is lost or stolen.

Revolving Line of Credit

Banks and some other financial institutions offer revolving lines of credit. This open account credit lets you write checks from regular checking accounts and certain designated credit line accounts.

They do not involve the use of credit cards, which is an asset because they are less expensive than traditional credit cards and they offer more credit.

With revolving lines of credit, people are able to borrow money and they are able to write checks. The three major types are:

- Overdraft protection lines
- Unsecured personal lines of credit
- Home equity credit lines

HOME EQUITY CREDIT LINE

A home equity line is similar to an unsecured personal credit line except that it is secured by a second mortgage on the home. This way, a consumer can tap into the home's equity without having to sell it. Most lenders will allow no more than 75 percent of the home's value for a home equity line of credit.

TAX CONCERN

If a homeowner itemizes tax deductions, the home equity loans interest charges of up to $100,000 can be deducted from taxes. However, this can only be done if the total indebtedness on the house is less than the fair market value of the house. It is not likely for this to be a problem since homeowners are not able to borrow more than 75 to 80 percent of the home's market value.

PREPAID CARD

A prepaid card is loaded with an amount of money that has already been supplied by the user; each time a purchase is made, that amount is deducted. Once the amount on the card is used up, the card can either be recharged or discarded. These cards are sometimes called smart cards or electronic purses, and can be plugged into a computer for verification and to avoid internet fraud. A prepaid card is similar to a debit card in that each use debits an amount rather than borrowing it.

OVERDRAFT PROTECTION LINE

An overdraft protection line is a checking account that offers a line of credit so that a customer who overdraws is protected up to a specified amount against a bounced check. Credit limits are often around $500-$1,000, but they can be thousands of dollars or more. Sometimes a credit card is tied to the checking account so that overdraft protection is funded by the credit card line and deposited it into the checking account to cover the overdraft.

UNSECURED PERSONAL CREDIT LINE

An unsecured personal credit line makes credit available on an as-needed basis. It's a way to borrow money from a bank, S&L, credit union, or brokerage firm without having to set up a new loan. The downside to an unsecured personal credit line is that large cash advances are readily available and as easy to access as using a credit card. A consumer needs to practice discipline with an unsecured personal line of credit.

CREDIT INVESTIGATION PROCESS

Once credit has been applied for, the information provided will be investigated by the issuer to determine if the applicant is credit-worthy.

Age, employment history, renting/owning a home, salary, debt and how that debt is being handled are key things that are reviewed. During the investigation, the lender tries to ensure that all of the information on the application is correct. Misleading information is cause for rejection.

CREDIT SCORING

Credit scoring assigns values to an applicant's home ownership, income, credit references, debts, savings, and the number and types of credit cards in order to determine if a person is credit-worthy. Fair Isaac & Co., the largest provider of credit scores, use only credit information to calculate their score. Their score is made up of five parts which include length of credit history (15 percent), payment history (35 percent), types of credit used (10 percent), new credit (10 percent), and amount owed (30 percent).

Credit Application Process

In order to receive charge cards, bank credit cards, or any type of revolving line of credit, a formal credit card application process must be undertaken. Issuing banks, stores, businesses, and companies all offer these applications. Information about employment, housing, and other current charge accounts and other debt must be provided. This information helps the issuer decide if the applicant is credit-worthy.

Credit Bureaus

Credit bureaus have come under fire in the past because errors were both frequent and unresolved. Recently, credit bureaus have adopted a more consumer-oriented approach which has helped improve their customer service and resolution of any disputes. In 1995, the Fair Credit Reporting Act was amended to provide credit reporting guidelines for the industry. Credit bureaus must now provide consumers with credit report copies and give toll-free numbers. Also, all disputes between creditors and consumers take both sides into account and must be resolved in thirty days.

ADB

Average Daily Balance (ADB) method applies interest charges to the average daily balance of an account over the billing period and in order to calculate finance charges. There are four types of ADB used by banks and retail charge card issuers, the most widely-used of which is ADB with new purchases. Under this method, outstanding balance (including new purchased) is tallied for each day in the billing cycle and then payments and credits are subtracted. This number is then divided by the number of days in the billing cycle. ADB excluding new purchases is figured in the same way except that it does not include new purchases. Two-cycle ADB including new purchases is also configured like the first method but it uses the average daily balance for the previous and the current billing cycles. Two-cycle ADB excluding new purchases is calculated the same as the two-cycle ADB method except that it does not include new purchases.

Monthly Credit Card Statement

Credit card statements show the billing cycle, payment due dates, interest rate, minimum payment, and all of the account activity for that period. Retail charge cards' monthly statements are similar but do not have a cash advance section. Lenders who offer revolving line of credit also send statements each month showing the borrowed amount, payments, and finance charges.

The credit card's account summary includes the previous balance, any new charges that were incurred in the past month, finance charges for any unpaid balance, the previous cycle's payment, credits for returns and refunds, and the new balance.

Credit Card Companies

Know your credit needs. If you are able to pay your account in full each month, look for ways you can reduce fees or earn rewards. If you carry balances month to month, look for a lower introductory rate. Look at your credit card's terms every six months and check out the card issuer's website to see if there are any incentives for new customers. If it's a better deal than what you have, ask the issuer for it. They may decide to offer you those terms in order to keep you as a customer. Check out credit card sites (such as www.bankrate.com) to compare offers from competing credit card companies.

Choosing a Credit Card

When choosing a credit card, it is important to consider a number of things. The first is the annual fee. Another is the interest rate, if it is fixed or variable, and if there is an introductory rate that will increase after a certain period of time. It is also good to ask what the grace period is before there is applied interest. Know if a late fee will be charged if payment is not made on time. Understand if there are to be any changes in your contract, how and when you will be contacted about them.

Avoid Credit Problems

To avoid credit problems, it is important to use restraint and discipline and to devise a good repayment plan. Do not accept every preapproved credit card offer that comes in the mail. Reduce the number of credit cards to one or two. Do not charge anything else on a credit card until the existing balance is paid off. Transfer any balances to a card with a low introductory rate and pay off as much as you can before the rate increases. All credit card debt should be consolidated and paid off as quickly as possible with a low-rate loan.

Special Types of Credit Cards

There are special types of credit cards that offer specific benefits, incentives, and rebates. One is the reward card. In addition to the traditional features of a bank card, it offers reward programs such as airline mileage or acquired points toward the purchase of an item. Student credit cards offer promotional programs that appeal to them such as discounts on movies, pizza, computer software, and so forth. Affinity cards are credit cards with a cause because they are issued in conjunction with a charity or political or professional group. Secured (collateralized) credit cards are cards that require collateral, such as a bank CD.

Credit Card Fraud

To reduce the chances of being the victim of credit card fraud, deal with legitimate retailers when using a credit card via the Internet. Only give credit card information over the telephone if you made the call, and try to restrict the use for retailers you know and trust. Do not put credit card information on checks, and do not put a telephone number, address, or Social Security number on credit/charge slips.

Keep your eye on the imprint when a clerk is ringing something up so no additional receipts are made. If the clerk makes a mistake, ask for the first imprint and tear it up immediately. Draw a line through any blank spaces above the total on a credit slip so that the amount can't be changed. The issuer of a lost or stolen credit card should be contacted immediately. Destroy all old carbons, credit slips, and cards, and go over your monthly statement promptly.

Personal Bankruptcy

Personal bankruptcy lets people who are in debt file a petition with a court to protect them from creditors and to make arrangements for liquidating and distributing their assets. Personal bankruptcy happens when the debt exceeds the ability to repay it. Illness, job loss, or simply living beyond one's means can result in bankruptcy. Missed payments drops a credit rating and property will be repossessed unless the problem is resolved. If it is not, bankruptcy may be the only choice.

Straight Bankruptcy

Straight bankruptcy permits the financial slate to be wiped clean. About 70 percent of personal bankruptcies are filed as straight bankruptcies. Straight bankruptcy does not rid a debtor of all obligations, but does allow assets to be retained. For example, a debtor may have to pay taxes or child support but can receive Social Security benefits. Equity in a home, a car, and other assets remain with the debtor. Federal or state regulations apply depending upon what the debtor's assets are. In general, state laws are more generous than federal laws concerning the assets a debtor can keep.

Wage Earner Plan

The Wage Earner Plan puts together a debt repayment schedule that works with a debtor's income. Individuals who are steadily employed, owe no more than $750,000 in secured debt and $250,000 in unsecured debt, and who can repay the debts in three to five years are good candidates for the plan. Creditors must agree to the plan; since they are likely to receive a larger amount than they would in a straight bankruptcy, most will agree. During the repayment period, interest charges

and late-payment penalties are dropped. After the plan is put in place, periodic payments are made to the court that then pays off the creditors. Throughout the process, the debtor retains assets and titles to properties.

Credit counselors

Credit counselors are professionals who help overextended consumers create budgets and repayment schedules. Some counselors collect money from consumers and pay creditors. In exchange for a fee, private credit counseling firms counsel clients and act as intermediaries between borrowers and creditors.

Nonprofit agencies

Nonprofit agencies like the Consumer Credit Counseling Services (CCCS) provide similar services for less. Be sure to check out the track record, fees, and provided services for any credit counselor before using them.

Major Purchases

Car-Buying Process

The first thing to do when buying a car is deciding how much you can afford. Decide if you will pay cash, finance, or lease. Narrow choices to a few that offer the performance, size, safety, and styling you desire. Take into consideration the dealer's cost, options, mark-up, rebates, and incentives. Used cars should inspected by a reputable mechanic not associated with the seller. Test-drive the car around town and on the highway.

Negotiate pricing with a few dealers before you close the deal. If trading in your old car, negotiate the price on the new car separate from the sale of the old car. Consider purchasing the car online. Do not feel pressured into buying extras you do not need. Finally, examine contract carefully with the dealer's finance manager and ask questions. Sign nothing unless you understand it fully.

Determine Your Budget

Unless you are able to pay cash, you'll need to determine the down payment as well as how much monthly payment you can afford. If the down payment will come out of savings, make sure you still have enough for emergencies. Budget enough money for insurance, maintenance and gas. The general rule of thumb is that monthly car payment should not exceed more than 20 percent of your monthly net income.

Operating Costs

In addition to the car payments, there are other out-of-pocket costs to consider such as insurance, gas, license, oil, tires, tune-ups, and repairs. Some of these costs will be fixed no matter how much you drive, while others will be variable depending on the number of miles you drive. Among the biggest fixed costs are monthly loan or lease payments; one of the biggest variable costs will be fuel for the car. Depreciation, or the car's loss in value over time, is another out-of-pocket cost.

Type of Car Needs

Think about your needs, likes, and dislikes when considering the size, body style, and features of a car you're considering buying. In general, the bigger the car, the more it costs to operate. Fuel economy, performance, appearance, reliability, repair problems, and resale value are other things to consider. Make a list of the things that you want and need and stick to it.

Reliability and Warranties

Consult car-buying guides such as Consumer Reports and talk to people you know who own the make and model you are thinking about buying. Compare warranties; they could differ greatly. You are guaranteed for general reliability and quality construction of a car for a certain amount of time (usually at least three years or 36,000 miles, whichever comes first), and the manufacturers will have to repair or replace defective parts at little or no cost to you. Be sure to read the fine print because most warranties do include qualifications and limitations.

Pros and Cons of Gas, Diesel, and Hybrid Cars

While diesel-powered vehicles offer better fuel economy than gasoline-powered vehicles, that advantage may be offset by the fact that diesel fuel costs more than gasoline. Hybrid cars blend gas and battery power and are increasingly popular due to their improved technology and steep gas prices. While more economical in terms of fuel, the cost of battery replacement is high and these cars typically have a substantially higher initial purchase price. Also, the fuel cost savings in hybrids will generally not justify the cost differential.

Buying a Used Car

A used car will not depreciate as rapidly as a new car. Because used cars are less expensive, the down payment will be lower. There are many low-mileage late-model used vehicles available because of the number of consumers who use short-term car leases. Because federal laws require sellers must sign a statement that the odometer is accurate, there should be no questions about accuracy.

The biggest disadvantage to buying a used car is the unknown of its mechanical condition. A car could have low mileage but have mechanical problems and expensive repairs in the future that cannot be determined during a test drive. If you are thinking of buying a used car, having it inspected by a good mechanic first is imperative.

Inspection

Before buying a car, note how easily you can open the car and get both yourself and your belongings in and out. Make sure the seat is comfortable and easy to adjust. Check gauges and blinds spots. Make sure that both trunk and seat fold-down options will work for the things you need to transport. Ensure that you can reach controls—heat, air, radio, CD, blinkers, headlights, wipers—easily while driving. Finally, check to see that the options you want are available.

Test-Driving a Car

When test-driving a car, try it out on the highways and local roads for at least twenty minutes apiece. Test the accelerator by merging onto the freeway and passing other cars. If you can, drive the car to your house to ensure that it will fit in your garage. Test the heater and air conditioner on a used car and turn the fan on and off, listening for engine noises that do not sound right. Test that gears shift smoothly and that the car handles well when parallel parking, making a U-turn, and braking hard.

Negotiation of Car Price

It is important to understand the dealer's cost for a new car in order to get a good price for it; the sticker price is far less important when it comes to negotiating. You can find the dealer's cost through Edmunds and Kelley Blue Book at www.edmunds.com, www.kbb.com, and www.autobytel.com. Beginning with the dealer's cost, aim for a firm quote for the lowest markup you can; let the sales person know you are comparison shopping. Having dealer cost information enhances bargaining power and may even help you get a price close to the dealer's cost.

Getting a Good Deal

To save money when buying a car, consult the Kelley Blue Book so that you know what the car is worth. Focus on this amount instead of the monthly payments and negotiate from the dealer's cost up instead of the sticker price down. After the price has been figured, do the math. If you're going to be trading in your old car, wait to negotiate it until after you've agreed on a firm price on the purchase. Shop at the end of the month; if sales people have not met their quotas, they may be more flexible. Take a careful look at paperwork to make sure items you don't want haven't been included. Finally, be ready to walk away; the dealer just may follow you and offer a better deal.

Closing the Deal

When purchasing a new or used car you will sign a contract agreeing to the price and conditions. Be sure that the car is exactly what you want and can afford because once both parties sign the contract it is legally binding. When you sign, you may be asked to give a small deposit (e.g. $300) as a gesture of good faith. Once the dealer accepts the offer, you can take possession of the car. If you do not have cash, you can work with a finance company, bank, the dealer, or a credit union for payment options. Before accepting the car, inspect it to make sure the dealer has cleaned it and taken care of any options that were agreed upon. Make sure you also receive the title.

Single-Family Homes and Condominiums

Single-family homes are the most popular type of housing that refers to any townhouse, row lot, or stand-alone home that shares a common wall. With single-family homes, owners have privacy, property control, prestige, and pride.

Condominiums (condos) are a kind of ownership, not a kind of building, and can be cluster housing, townhouses, or apartments. Condo owners have a title, mortgage, and title to their own unit and part ownership of common areas and amenities. They also pay a monthly homeowner fee for their part of the common facility maintenance costs, and there is a homeowners' association which elects a board of people to take care of the buildings and common areas. The pros of condos are that they cost less than single-family housing and also do not have as much maintenance responsibility.

Cooperative Apartments

With cooperative apartments, each tenant owns a part of the non-profit corporation that owns the building where the tenant lives. Tenants lease their units from the corporation and pay monthly fees depending on their space and ownership share. The fees take care of the cost of services, maintenance, taxes, and the building's mortgage, but are subject to change with actual operating costs and decisions made by the board of directors. The downside to cooperative apartments is that rent can increase if there are empty units and it can be difficult to get a mortgage. Also, if the board decides to make capital improvements, fees can increase.

Economic and Emotional Factors

Three factors that influence the economics of renting or buying a place to live are homeowners' tax write-offs, mortgage interest rates and housing prices, and the decrease or increase over time in home values. It's also important to look at the general state of the housing market as well as individual needs. Renting may make more sense if the buyer expects to relocate within a couple of years. The desire for privacy, the ability to personalize a home, and the pride of home ownership may support buying over renting.

Financial Payoffs to Home Ownership

Two major financial reasons for owning a home are as an inflation hedge and a tax shelter. An inflation hedge occurs when a home appreciates in value at the same or greater rate than inflation. A tax shelter requires that deductions be itemized. Since property taxes and mortgage interest can be deducted when doing federal (and often state) income taxes, your tax liability is reduced when taxable income is lessened.

PMI

Private mortgage insurance (PMI) is a policy that protects a lender from loss if the borrower defaults on the loan. Lenders usually want a PMI when a down payment is less than 20 percent. For example, if a borrower makes a 10 percent down payment, the mortgage is a 90 percent loan with mortgage insurance covering 10 percent of the price of the home. Mortgage insurance is usually about .50 percent with the average cost running about $40 to $70 per month. Once the equity in your home is at 20 to 25 percent, you should get in touch with your lender to cancel the mortgage insurance.

READY FOR HOME OWNERSHIP SIGNS

If you have had a steady income and job history for at least the last two years you may be qualified to buy a home; if you have not, figure out how the gaps can be explained and work to improve the situation. If you have saved money for a down payment and closing costs, have good credit, and have a good track record of repaying debts on time, these are good signs that you can handle the financial responsibility of buying and owning a home. Finally, if you can afford the monthly mortgage payments for the house that you want, you may be ready to buy.

DOWN PAYMENT WHEN BUYING A HOME

The down payment is that portion of a home's purchase price that the buyer pays in cash upon purchasing. It is often referred to as equity. Most home buyers have to save for several years in order to have enough for a down payment and other costs of buying and owning a home, so it is important to save and invest early and wisely if home ownership is a financial goal. One source for money to cover a down payment is to take it from your company's profit-sharing plan or an IRA, but using retirement money should be a last resort because income tax must still be paid on retirement distributions.

MORTGAGE POINTS

Mortgage points are fees that lenders charge when they grant a mortgage loan. These points relate directly to the demand for mortgages and the lender's supply of loanable funds; the greater the demand, the more points you'll have to pay. One point is equivalent to 1 percent of the amount borrowed. Points allow lenders to adjust interest rates to suit a buyer's needs. Points paid on a mortgage at the time of home purchase are tax deductible; however, if points incurred during a refinance are not.

HOME-BUYING PROCESS

Most homebuyers begin by previewing the market via Internet, word of mouth or newspaper ads. Make a list of desirable features, but keep an open mind as finding a home that perfectly suits a wish-list isn't easy. Hire a real estate agent who can help you negotiate price, get good financing, and help prepare the contract. Meet with a mortgage lender to prearrange a mortgage loan. Finally, review the sales contract with your agent and close the deal.

LOAN PREQUALIFICATION ADVANTAGES

Prequalification allows a lender to consider a buyer's circumstance and predict the kind of loan the buyer will be eligible for. This helps a homebuyer focus the search on that price range. Prequalification also offers down payment and closing cost estimates for different kinds of mortgages, and helps identify any application problems early on (e.g. credit report error) so that they can be corrected. Finally, prequalification gives a potential seller confidence that the prospective house buyer can afford the property and will be able to get proper financing.

MORTGAGE LOAN

A mortgage loan is a loan made for the purchase of a property, with the property as collateral. Mortgage loans can be obtained through commercial banks, thrift institutions, mortgage brokers, and credit unions. The two most common types of mortgage loans are fixed rate mortgages, in which the interest rate and monthly payment are fixed for the full term of the loan, and adjustable rate mortgages, in which the interest rate and monthly payment are adjusted according to market rate movements.

REAL ESTATE AGENT

Real estate agents know the market, have already been inside many homes that might be just what you're looking for, and are trained to manage the offer-counteroffer process. The can guide buyers toward reputable lenders, inspectors and other professionals. Real estate agents are usually paid by the sellers, even when they are hired as buyers' representatives. Agents are paid through their brokers, and brokers only receive payment if the sale closes. Commissions are arranged between seller and listing broker, but generally range between 5 and 7 percent. Since real estate transactions are legally and financially complex, it is recommended to use a Realtor instead of trying to buy a property that is for sale by owner.

CLOSING ON A HOME

Avoid major purchases prior to closing on the home. If the purchase is urgent, discuss it with the loan officer. Don't leave or change jobs prior to closing, as the lender will likely check this just prior to closing. Allow your agent to handle all communication with the seller. Put earnest money deposit to a for-sale-by-owner seller in a trust account. Alert the utility companies about your move-in date. Follow the lender's requirements to the letter. Don't be overly concerned if the appraisal comes in low; that doesn't necessarily mean the home's value is lower than your agreed-upon price. Your agent may be able to provide information to the appraiser that shows the home's value in a better light. While agents aren't required to be at the closing, ask yours to accompany you to help smooth any glitches.

ARM

Basic features of an adjustable rate mortgage (ARM) include the adjustment period, the interest rate, payment caps and interest rate caps. The adjustment period is typically six months to a year, although it can be anywhere from three months to three years; The ARM's interest rate is arrived at by adding the index or baseline rate to the margin. Payment caps are the limits placed on payment increases resulting from a rate adjustment. Interest rate caps are the limits on how much an interest rate can increase over a certain time period.

RENT-TO-OWN

Even though a low weekly price may seem reasonable, rent-to-own is an expensive option that often results in paying two to four times retail cost. In general, carrying a balance for a short time on a low-rate credit card is less costly than rent-to-own. Payments not made on time will result in late fees. A better option than rent-to-own is to save the money needed over a period of time to purchase the item in full.

MAJOR APPLIANCE PURCHASE

When purchasing a major appliance, look at the general appearance, including color, style, size, material, quality. Make sure it will work for your needs, fit the spot, and look acceptable once it's there. Consider an Energy Star model to save utilities costs, fuel, and clothing, and may result in a tax break. Read ads and brochure information carefully for function, capacity, and any other performance-related information. Review the warranty; make sure you're clear on what is covered and what isn't. Call the manufacturer with any questions. Try to visit a store that has the appliance on display. Open doors, inspect features, and make sure the appliance is well-made.

Major Appliance Shopping

When shopping for a major appliance, ask yourself:

- What features do I want? Consult Consumer Reports or the Internet for customer reviews, ratings, and opinions. Major appliance stores such as Best Buy, Sears, Home Depot, and Lowe's are a good place to start looking
- When do I need to have it? The best time to look for a new appliance is before an old model gives out so that you don't have to hurry into a purchase. Take some time to research so that you can get the best price
- Would I consider buying second-hand? Decide if the new factor outweighs the cost
- What is my price range? Know the price range of the appliance and the various features available at both low and high ends

Purchasing Furniture

When purchasing furniture here are some things to keep in mind:

- Know how much you can spend. Set a budget and stick to it
- Know your needs. Determine what you need and how long you will use it
- Know how it will be used. Consider style, construction, and materials that suit your lifestyle. People with children or pets may need more durable, stain-resistant options than those without pets or children
- Measure room dimensions, and keep in mind the widths of stairs, halls, and doorways to make sure the furniture will fit
- Understand furniture types and terms. This includes woods, finishes, upholstered furniture, frames, and supports
- Know when to shop. Plan in advance to take advantage of seasonal sales, clearances, discontinued or display models
- Know where to shop. Visit furniture stores and department stores and shop around for quality, price, credit terms, service, and delivery terms
- Read labels. Read all of the seller and manufacturer's labels and tags
- Understand warranties and returns. Get specifics in writing

Big-Ticket Purchases

Some guidelines for big ticket purchases are to:

- Create a short-term savings plan for items that cost less than a few thousand dollars
- Use store layaway plans to put aside merchandise that is a good price or store financing plans that don't need immediate payment so that you can save before your payment is due
- Set aside unexpected extra money, such as a tax refund or bonus, for big ticket items
- Compare at least three retailers for pricing on the item, and do research on the Internet
- Shop during peak sales times (e.g. after Christmas) and review issues of Consumer Reports for product reviews, ratings, and recommendations
- Think about purchasing extended warranties for some big ticket items such as exercise equipment (e.g. elliptical and treadmills), laptops, and plasma TVs as these items have a higher chance of needing repairs within three years; most warranties only cover items for a year or less. Be wary of purchasing extended warranties for other items that probably won't need them

Taxes

TAXES

Taxes are our dues to society. By taxing citizens on the federal, state, and local tax levels, governments provide public services and activities from schools and libraries to national defense. The average family pays about one-third of its gross income in federal income, Social security, property, sales, state, and local taxes. Tax planning helps minimize the amount of taxes that must be paid by keeping aware of all possible deductions.

MANDATORY PAYROLL TAXES

There are some mandatory payroll taxes that every employee must have taken out of the paycheck according to the law. The employers then turn these withholdings over to different tax agencies. If an employer does not turn over these withholdings, they may be assessed a Trust Fund Recovery Penalty by the IRS and pay 100 percent of the taxes plus interest. In general, payroll tax deductions usually include state, federal, Social Security, and Medicare. A variety of local tax withholdings such as county, city, county, or school district taxes may be withheld as well.

FICA

FICA stands for the Federal Insurance Contributions Act and oversees the collection of payroll taxes for Social Security benefits. The FICA tax is made up of both Social Security and Medicare taxes; both are split evenly between employee and the employer. FICA taxes are usually collected at a rate of 7.65 percent on gross earnings (earnings before any deductions). The total FICA tax adds up to 15.3 percent and breaks down as the employer and employee each pay 6.2 percent for Social Security and the employer and employee each paying 1.45 percent apiece for Medicare.

RED FLAGS

Some red flags that could trigger an audit include either incorrectly reported income or a large increase in income. If there are any errors such as miscalculations or missing forms, signatures, or Social Security numbers, a red flag may be waved. Owning a small business and/or taking a deduction for a home office could also raise a red flag; itemizing deductions higher than average for your bracket of income could also place you at risk for an audit as well as could any casualty losses. Finally, if your reported income is lower than what the 1099 Form shows, you could also be in jeopardy of being audited.

VOLUNTARY PAYROLL DEDUCTIONS

Voluntary payroll deductions are deductions that an employee agrees to have withheld from paychecks for certain benefits or programs that the employee wants to participate in. These deductions can be paid with pre-tax dollars or after-tax dollars, depending on the benefit type. Voluntary payroll deductions can include health insurance (including medical, dental, and vision), life insurance, retirement plan contributions (e.g.401k plan), stock options, and products, services, and other work-related perks and expenses.

TAXPAYING TIPS

To make taxpaying easier, file taxes on time even if you can't pay what you owe. If you can't pay your whole bill, pay in installments. If you file for an extension, pay what you think you'll owe. Remember to include any tax-free income like tuition or inheritance, and remember to sign your return (even if you file online). If you have made charitable gifts that aren't cash and are valued at more than $500, include the receipts with Form 8283. Finally, if you use direct deposit, you'll receive your refund more quickly.

Economics of Income Taxes

Income taxes are the federal government's largest source of revenue. Personal income taxes are done on a progressive tax structure, which means the more money you make, the higher the rate at which it will be taxed. The marginal tax rate is the rate you pay on the next dollar of taxable income, and the average tax rate is the rate each dollar of taxable income will be taxed on average. If you relate the tax liability to the level of taxable income earned, the average tax rate will be lowered considerably.

IRS Assists a Taxpayer

Aside from issuing guides to help people prepare their tax returns, the IRS can help calculate taxes for people who have a taxable income of less than $100,000 and do not itemize deductions. In order to use this service, certain information must be supplied along with a signed and dated tax return that is mailed to the IRS on or before the April 15 deadline of the year that immediately follows the tax year. The IRS tries to help the taxpayer accurately figure taxes owed. If the taxpayer's withheld too much, the IRS will issue a refund, and if not enough was withheld, the IRS will send a bill for the amount owed.

Computer-Based Tax Returns

If a taxpayer wants to itemize deductions without tax advice, special tax preparation computer software can help. Software saves time in filling out forms by saving data to plug into other forms, and can also remind the taxpayer about deductions that haven't been included. There is computer software for both tax planning and tax preparation. Programs such as Quicken help taxpayers use different strategies to see the effects on the amount of taxes they must pay. Software programs are updated each year to include any tax law changes.

Categories of Tax Filing Status

Single tax filing status refers to an unmarried person or someone who is legally separated. Married filing jointly is for married couples who combine their incomes and deductions and file one tax return. Married filing separately refers to a married couple where each separately files and claims income, deductions, and exemptions. Head of household status is for an individual who pays more than half of the cost of maintaining a home for an eligible dependent. Qualifying widow or widower with a dependent child refers to someone whose spouse died within two years of the tax year and who supports a dependent child.

Private Tax Preparers

People use private tax preparers because preparing taxes can be time-consuming and intimidating. Professional tax preparers are knowledgeable about minimizing tax liability. There are local and national tax services, such as independent local firms and companies like H&R Block. If your taxes are pretty straightforward, this is a good service. CPAs are professional tax preparers who take care of returns and counsel taxpayers on planning. Enrolled agents have to pass a two-day; IRS-administered test and are federally licensed and able to handle complex tax preparation. Tax attorneys are lawyers who specialize in tax planning.

Tax Evasion and Tax Avoidance

Tax evasion is the intentional failure to report income or pay taxes altogether and is illegal. There are severe financial penalties and possible prison terms for violators. Tax avoidance is a legal way of reducing taxes in keeping with Congress's objective. People who attempt to avoid paying tax feel that they are above the law and should not have to pay taxes are sometimes called tax protesters. A successful tax protester avoids tax while an unsuccessful protester tries to evade tax.

Pay-as-you-go Taxpaying System

Under the pay-as-you-go system, an employer deducts a part of your income each pay period and sends it to the IRS periodically. If you are self-employed, it is your responsibility to deduct a portion of your income each pay period and send it to the IRS at least four times a year. The amounts coincide with what the taxpayer's tax liability is estimated to be. At the end of the taxable year, your actual taxes need to be figured and a tax return filed. After filing, you will receive full credit for the amount of taxes deducted from your income during the taxable year, and will either receive a refund or owe money if you did not pay enough.

Federal Withholding Taxes

Employees complete a W-4 form to determine how much federal income tax should be taken out of each pay period's gross earnings. This form is based on the employee's income and asks whether the employee has multiple jobs or a spouse who also earns employment income. This form also incorporates the child and other dependent tax credits to which an employee might be entitled. Lastly, the employee is permitted to include extra income or deductions in the withholding calculation, and can request additional withholdings on top of that.

Taxable Income

Taxable income is the amount of taxable income and is figured by subtracting deductions, exemptions, and adjustments from gross income. The IRS has restrictions on what expenses can be deducted.

Gross Income

Gross income is total taxable income before deductions, adjustments, or exemptions. Gross income includes salaries, wages, bonuses, tips, commissions, alimony, lottery winnings, money from asset sales, and income from businesses, farms, pensions, annuities, rents, and partnerships.

Capital Gain

If an asset such as stocks or real estate is sold for a higher price than what it was purchased for, a capital gain occurs. For example, a stock purchased at $45 a share and sold for $65 a share would have a capital gain of $20 per share. Capital gains have different tax rates depending on the holding period; they are limited as to the amount in capital losses they can have in a given year, as specified by the IRS. A taxpayer can write off any capital losses against any capital gains.

Qualifying for a Special Allowance and Additional Withholding Allowance

A taxpayer who is single and has only one job or is married to a nonworking spouse may qualify for a special allowance. Additionally, if the taxpayer's wages from a second job or a spouse's wages are less than $1,000, they can also qualify. If a taxpayer is the head of household, has a large number of deductions, or has at least $1,500 of claimable child or dependent care expenses, an additional withholding allowance may be granted.

Individual Income Classifications

Individual income can be classified as portfolio, active, or passive. All of these have limitations on the number of deductions or write-offs a taxpayer can use. Portfolio income comes from investment earnings like bonds, stocks, savings accounts, and mutual funds. Active income is income earned through employment, like salaries, wages, bonuses, tips, and commissions. Noninvestment income like pensions and alimony also fall under this category. Passive income is that earned from limited partnerships and real estate as well as other types of tax shelters.

Adjustments to Gross Income

Adjustments to gross income are deductions allowed from gross income and can include employee, insurance, retirement, and support expenses. Most of these deductions are non-business and include paid alimony and self-employment taxes (limited to 50 percent of the amount paid) as well as some moving expenses, educator expenses, and IRA contributions. Other deductions include insurance payments for those who are self-employed and early withdrawal of savings penalties. After you have subtracted all of the allowable adjustments to your gross income, you are left with adjusted gross income (AGI). It is important to know the AGI value because it determines the limits for certain itemized deductions.

Standard Deductions and Itemized Deductions

A standard deduction is a fixed dollar amount based upon filing status, age, and whether or not you are blind and is used when a taxpayer's total itemized deductions are too small. Itemized deductions are specific personal expenses allowed to be deducted. Some of the more common non-business items that can be deducted include moving, dental, and medical expenses, as well as state and local personal property taxes and state, local, and foreign income and property taxes. Investment interest and residential mortgage interest also qualify, as do theft and casualty loss and charitable contributions.

Exemptions

Exemptions are the deductions from adjusted gross income depending on how many people a taxpayer's income supports. Personal exemptions can only be claimed once. A taxpayer can claim one exemption, another for a spouse, and additional exemptions for any dependents. Dependents are defined as children or other relatives who earn less than a certain level of income and for whom the taxpayer provides more than half of their support. This level of income is waived for full-time students who are under the age of twenty-four. Taxpayers with high levels of adjusted gross income will either have exemptions phased out or completely eliminated.

Tax Credit

A tax credit is a deduction that a taxpayer is allowed which reduces the taxes owed. These tax credits include adoption, foreign, disabled or elderly, mortgage interest, qualified electric vehicle, and child and dependent care expenses. One can also receive credit for the prior year's minimum tax. To receive one of these tax credits, the taxpayer has to file a return that includes a separate schedule showing what the claimed tax credit is.

Tax Form

The IRS requires that taxpayers use certain forms for filing returns; these forms and instruction booklets for preparing them are free to taxpayers.

1040EZ Form

A 1040EZ is a simple tax return form for taxpayers under the age of sixty-five who are single or married filing a joint return who do not have any dependents to claim and are not blind. Additionally, the taxable income must be less than $100,000 only from salaries, tips, wages, or taxable grants or scholarships, interest income less than $1,500, and no income adjustments, tax credits, or itemized deductions are being claimed.

TAX FILING CONSIDERATIONS

When filling out and filing tax forms, decide if will do the taxes yourself using computer software of if you will hire a tax professional to do your taxes. Then, determine if you need to file for an extension or if you will need to amend the return. Consider whether or not there is the potential of being audited, and if you will need to pay estimated taxes.

ESTIMATED TAXES

Estimated taxes are the taxes from income sources other than employment in which federal taxes are withheld. Estimated taxes must be paid by investors, consultants, lawyers, and business owners on income that has not been subject to withholding.

FILING EXTENSION

You can receive a filing extension for your federal tax return after the April 15 deadline without being hit with penalties as long as your extension is approved by the IRS, and you've paid sufficient estimated taxes; submitting a 4868 form results in an automatic four month extension, making the new due date August 15. Keep in mind this extension does not give you more time to pay taxes.

AMENDED RETURN

If a mistake has been made in taxes that have been filed, an amended return can be filed to correct the error. An amended return corrects the income or deductions and the taxes that should have been paid. An amended return can be filed within three years from the original filing date or two years from the date the taxes were paid (whichever is later).

TAX PLANNING STRATEGIES

There are a number of tax planning strategies that can help reduce a tax bill. Giving family members gifts of income-producing property or creating custodial accounts or trusts will move part of the income into a lower tax bracket. Maximizing deductions will also lower the tax bill. Finally, tax-deferred and tax-free income will also save money. Tax-deferred (or delayed) income means that this income is not currently being taxed, but will be at some point in the future. Most investments are tax-deferred, but some are tax-free, such as income from municipal bonds.

Insurance

Concept of Risk

In terms of insurance, risk is the uncertainty of economic loss. When a financial interest such as health, home, car, or business is lost or damaged, financial loss occurs. Anticipating and protecting against potential risks will protect you financially. Risk avoidance, loss prevention and control, risk assumption, and insurance can help prepare for risk.

Risk Avoidance

Risk avoidance is simply steering clear of situations that involve an increased level of danger. Some risk, however, is necessary. For example, if you avoid driving, your chances of being injured or killed in a car accident are reduced, but the inconvenience of not being able to drive may cause stress which can impact health. It is important to evaluate if avoiding the risk is potentially less harmful than taking the risk and its potential consequences.

Loss Prevention and Loss Control

Loss prevention lowers the likelihood that a loss will occur. For example, driving a car during good weather versus during a blizzard reduces the likelihood of being in a car accident.

Loss control reduces the impact of a loss when it occurs. For example, wearing a seatbelt or having a car with airbags reduces the chance of injury or death in an accident. Both loss prevention and loss control are important to risk management programs and allow insurance companies to handle risk reasonably.

Insurance Policy

An insurance policy is a legal agreement between the insured and the insurer in which the insurance company agrees to reimburse the insured for a certain level of loss according to policy. In exchange for premium payments, the insurance company will reimburse a percentage of the insured's loss under specified circumstances.

Insurance companies use actuarial data to estimate the potential risk of loss for an insured population. It is easier to predict losses for a group of policyholders than an individual, and accurately estimating the size and amount of insured losses is how insurance companies make money.

Underwriting

Through underwriting, insurance companies decide whom they will insure and at what rates. Through the underwriting process, insurance companies put together rate-classification schedules; premiums rise when the chance of loss is greater. Underwriters try to avoid adverse selection by preventing high-risk clients from getting coverage. It can be difficult for underwriters to figure out what the best classifying criteria is for potential purchasers.

Benefits to Life Insurance

There are important financial benefits of life insurance including financial protection for dependents, creditor protection, tax benefits, and savings. The most important benefit is providing for dependents upon your death. Creditor protection is important because creditors cannot claim cash benefits even if the deceased has outstanding debts and bills if the life insurance policy is set up to pay a beneficiary directly instead of through the estate. Life insurance payouts made to dependents aren't usually subject to state or federal income taxes, and sometimes dependents do not have to pay estate taxes if specific requirements are met. Finally, some life insurance policies can be used as savings vehicles.

MULTIPLE-OF-EARNINGS METHOD

The multiple-of-earnings method multiplies the gross annual earnings by a certain number to estimate how much insurance coverage is needed. Though a simple method, it is not entirely accurate and only gives a rough approximation of life insurance needs.

NEEDS ANALYSIS METHOD

The needs analysis method takes into account five different components for assessing a family's total economic needs.

1. The first is how much income the dependents will need in order to live comfortably. Looking at a family's current monthly budget for housing, utilities, food, clothing, medical/dental needs, property taxes, insurance, recreation/travel, and savings is helpful
2. Special needs of a dependent that is chronically ill or disabled, is attending college or has another special circumstance is the second component to consider
3. The third component involves extra expenses such as funeral costs or childcare costs if a surviving spouse reenters the workforce
4. Liquidity is important so that payouts from the policy can be used to pay bills
5. It is important to figure out how much would be needed to pay outstanding bills in order to leave a family debt-free

The needs analysis method looks at financial resources and obligations of the insured party and their dependents, and is far more precise and detailed. The needs analysis method determines a family's total economic need and what financial resources will be available after the insured party's death, and subtracts these resources from the financial need to determine how much life insurance is required.

FINANCIAL RESOURCES:

Financial resources not related to a life insurance policy include money from savings, investments, and Social Security survivor's benefits. Another resource may be payouts from the deceased employer's group life insurance or earned income from a surviving spouse and children. Additionally, many families have real estate, jewelry, stocks, bonds, and other assets that could be sold. It is important to put together a complete list of these resources and their values and update this list frequently.

TERM LIFE INSURANCE

Term life insurance is the simplest kind of insurance because a certain amount of insurance is purchased to cover a set period of protection. If the purchaser dies during that time period, the beneficiaries will receive everything specified in the policy. Term life insurance can be purchased for different time periods and premiums can be paid quarterly, semiannually, or annually.

The two types of term insurance are a straight term policy and a decreasing term policy. A straight term policy covers a set number of years; the amount of life insurance coverage stays the same. A decreasing term policy keeps the premium the same throughout the coverage period but the amount of protection decreases over the life of the policy. This is done because the possibility of death increases with age.

ADVANTAGES AND DISADVANTAGES

The biggest advantage of term life insurance is lower initial premiums than other types of insurance, especially for younger people. Term life insurance is an affordable way to get a greater degree of protection for a specific period of time.

The biggest disadvantage to term life insurance is that it only offers temporary coverage; once the policy term expires, the policy has to be renewed. Future underwriting factors can make it a challenge to qualify for insurance, but some term life policies offset this with a renewability provision which gives the policy holder the opportunity to renew without proof of insurability. There may also be a convertibility provision which allows the policy holder to convert term insurance policy to a comparable whole life policy in the future.

WHOLE LIFE INSURANCE

Whole life insurance provides ongoing insurance coverage for the insured's entire life. It also offers cash value, which is a small return on the investment. This cash value is obtained from investment earnings from premiums that have been paid. Savings rates on whole life policies are usually capped at a certain rate. The longer the policy is kept active, the greater the cash value.

ADVANTAGES AND DISADVANTAGES

Some of the advantages to whole life insurance are that individuals save regularly with periodic payments and there are tax breaks for these earnings. Premium payments can be budgeted over a long time, making them more affordable and eliminating the possibility of being denied life insurance at a later point in time. Premium payments contribute toward the insured's estate regardless of lifespan. However, whole life insurance does not provide yields as high as other investment types and offer less death insurance per premium dollar than term life insurance.

CONTINUOUS PREMIUM WHOLE LIFE POLICY

With continuous premium whole life policy, also called straight life, a level premium is paid every year until death or a nonforfeiture right is claimed. The younger the purchaser, the lower the premium will be. Although premiums are reduced by purchasing a policy at a younger age, the longer coverage period can mean a higher overall payment. Continuous premium insurance provides the highest amount of permanent death protection plus the lowest amount of savings per premium dollar, so it is a good choice for permanent life insurance.

LIMITED PAYMENT WHOLE LIFE POLICY

A limited payment whole life policy provides coverage over the course of the insured's entire life, but the premium payment is for a specified period. If there are age provisions (e.g. paid up to age fifty-five or sixty-five), premiums are paid up until that age. Some insurance companies try to persuade consumers that they will save money because they do not have to pay premiums over a lifetime. However, this is not entirely true: First, the purpose of whole life insurance is permanent protection against financial loss in the event of death. It is not meant to be a savings account. Second, if the goal of the life insurance is permanent coverage, a person should buy continuous premium whole life instead of the limited payment policy.

SINGLE PREMIUM WHOLE LIFE POLICIES

A single premium whole life policy is purchased with a one-time cash payment at the beginning of the contract with coverage for life. Its investment components are attractive to those who want a tax-sheltered investment vehicle. Any policy interest and investment earnings are tax deferred, but there is a 10 percent early withdrawal penalty. Also, there is a capital gains tax if cash withdrawals or loans are taken against the single premium whole life policy before age 59 ½.

DIFFERENT INSURANCE COMPANY OWNERSHIP

Depending on how a life insurance company's ownership is structured, there can considerable differences in insurance policy premiums. For all intents and purposes, the policy holders of a mutual company own the company. If mutual companies are managed well, policy holders receive income or periodic dividends that reduce their premiums.

Shareholders of stock companies own the company but they may or may not own policies, and they directly receive any dividends paid. Because of the difference in ownership types, the policy premiums for stock companies should be lower than those issued by mutual companies.

UNIVERSAL LIFE INSURANCE

Universal life insurance is a permanent cash value insurance that combines death benefits with a tax-sheltered savings/investment account that pays interest; this interest is usually paid at a competitive money market rate. Some of the premium pays administrative fees; the remainder is added to the cash value of the policy where it earns a return rate. Although this earnings rate varies with market yields, there is a guaranteed minimum rate. As long as there is enough in the savings part to cover death protection, the policy will remain in effect. If the cash value becomes very large, insurance coverage must be increased in order for the policy to keep its favorable tax treatment.

ADVANTAGES AND DISADVANTAGES

One advantage of universal life insurance is savings, because the policy is credited at the current rate of interest. Another advantage is flexibility, because the cost of death protection is covered with an annual premium. One disadvantage is that protection levels and premiums can change. A policy holder may have to pay higher premiums down the line if early premium payments were economized. Another disadvantage is fees and charges. The first premium has a front-end load or commission, and there are fees for each annual premium, plus investment expenses and other charges.

MEDICAL EXAM FOR A LIFE INSURANCE POLICY

When buying life insurance, be honest about your medical history; insurance companies can and do check into medical backgrounds. You may be asked to take a medical exam before the insurance policy will be approved. Before taking an exam, do not drink alcohol or caffeine or smoke or chew tobacco in the hours before the exam. Also, avoid strenuous exercise for twenty-four hours prior to the exam, which may be done in your home or office by a paramedical professional who may take blood, urine, and saliva samples to test for HIV, cholesterol, diabetes, and other health issues. If you are purchasing a large policy or are more than forty, an EKG or X-rays may be required as well as a treadmill test.

TYPES OF LIFE INSURANCE

Some other types of life insurance include variable, group, and special purpose. Variable life insurance means benefits are directly tied to the returns on investments made by the policy holder. Under group life insurance each eligible member of the group receives an insurance certificate for an overall, master policy for everyone in the group. Special purpose insurance can include credit life (life insurance sold along with installment loans), mortgage life (mortgage balance is paid off if the borrower dies), and industrial life insurance (policies with small face amounts, often less than $1,000).

Property Insurance

Property insurance protects real and personal property against natural and manmade catastrophes such as tornadoes, fire, hail, theft, and vandalism. Property insurance lists both the property and the types of destructive acts (perils) that are covered.

In order to receive property insurance the owner needs to compile a comprehensive list of specific property to be insured. It may be necessary to include appraisals with this list. The more specific this list is, the easier it is to settle a claim. Second, a purchaser must decide on the types of perils property needs to be protected against.

Liability Insurance

Liability insurance protects against financial burden in the event the insured is responsible for accidental injury or property loss to someone else. This insurance helps cover legal fees to in the event the insured is sued, although should the accident be determined to be the result of negligence caused by the insured's failure to act in a responsible manner, the insurance will not pay.

Home Insurance Costs Factors

Home insurance costs can be affected by risk factors that pose a hazard such as trampolines, swimming pools, and even certain pets. The construction materials used on a home also affects insurance costs, brick and Hardiplank homes cost less to insure than those built of wood. The age and style of the house also are figured into the costs. Finally, the location of the home affects insurance costs. Insurance premiums for all homeowners will be higher if there are a large number of claims filed from in area (e.g. high-crime level areas).

PAP

A Personal automobile policy (PAP) is a comprehensive insurance policy for automobile owners and is intended to be easily understood by a typical insurance purchaser. It has six parts, with the first four identifying the type of coverage provided:

- Liability coverage (Part A)
- medical payments coverage (Part B)
- uninsured motorists coverage (Part C)
- coverage for damage to your vehicle (Part D)
- (Part E) explains the duties and responsibilities in the event of an accident
- (Part F) outlines the basic provisions of the policy, including policy coverage period and right of termination

Supplemental Property Insurance Coverage

Not all types of damage are covered by homeowner's policies, so it is important to decide if you need any type of supplemental coverage. Some common types of supplemental coverage include flood insurance, earthquake insurance, and transportation insurance. In 1968, the federal government established a subsidized flood insurance program to work with private insurance to offer lower-cost flood insurance coverage in certain areas.

Under this program, land-use controls are put in place to help reduce future flood losses. With earthquake insurance, a 15 percent deductible on the replacement cost of a home that is destroyed or damaged by an earthquake is required. Besides car insurance, an individual may want to insure vehicles such as motorcycles, boats, RVs, mobile homes, and personal watercrafts.

Renter's Insurance

Even if the building being rented is insured, anything that you own in that building is not. Renter's insurance covers losses due to fire, lightning, explosion, windstorms, hail, theft, civil commotion, aircraft, vehicles, smoke, vandalism, falling objects, building collapse, and the weight of water and snow.

A standard policy takes care of carpets, furniture, appliances, clothing, electronic equipment, and other personal items at their value at the time of loss. Renter's insurance premiums are dependent upon location, but are generally very affordable. You can also purchase replacement cost insurance, which pays to fully replace lost items with new ones.

Property Insurance Premiums

Insurance companies base their premiums on the amount of risk they perceive and the potential for losses. Limit potential hazards to lower premiums. Have good lighting around property to minimize the likelihood of someone falling, and to ward off potential thieves.

Make sure that electrical wiring, stairways, carpeting and flooring are in good shape to avoid accidents. Swimming pools need to be secured with fences and locks, and should be covered or drained when not in use. Keep valuables in a safe deposit box and do not keep valuables or a lot of cash at home. Take photos of insured items and keep detailed records, including appraisals.

Private Health Insurance

Private health insurance plans are offered to both individuals and groups. These plans are either traditional indemnity plans or managed care plans. With traditional indemnity plans, healthcare services are obtained from someone other than the insurer; the insurer reimburses a portion of payments when a claim is submitted, or they pay the health service provider directly.

With managed care plans, certain organizations or individual providers are contracted to provide services for a monthly fee. These plans include HMOs, PPOs, EPOs, and similar plans. It is estimated that private health insurance pays for about 35 percent of medical expenses in the United States.

Government Health Insurance Programs

About 25 percent of the US population is covered under some type of government health insurance program. Medicare, administered by Social Security, is one of these programs and is paid for with social security taxes of covered workers and their employers. Medicare provides basic hospital insurance and supplementary medical insurance. Medicaid is a state-run public assistance program which provides health insurance benefits for those who are not able to afford health insurance.

Worker's compensation insurance is another government health insurance plan that compensates workers who are injured on the job or become ill from work-related causes.

Choosing a Healthcare Plan

When choosing a healthcare plan, it is important to what the plan will cost each month and co-pays for doctors outside the plan's network. Understanding out-of-pocket limits in the case of a major illness or injury is essential. Review doctors, hospitals, services, and other medical providers covered under the plan. Know the deductibles you have to pay before insurance kicks in to help cover the costs.

Disability Insurance Needs

To estimate your disability needs, figure take-home pay (disability benefits are usually tax-free so you'll only need to replace your take-home pay). Policies paid by employers are either partially or fully taxable. Figure out the monthly disability amount you will receive from Social Security, other government programs, company disability benefits, and group disability policy benefits and subtract your existing monthly disability benefits from it. This will give you an idea of the monthly disability benefits needed.

Saving on Disability Income Insurance

Some ways to save on disability income insurance include reducing premiums by extending waiting periods, getting a policy that has benefits to age sixty-five instead of a lifetime, asking about premium discounts for prepaying, and requesting that recurring medical problems (e.g. back problems) be excluded. Get a number of price quotes since rates can vary, and check with your employer to see if disability insurance is offered as a benefit. Think about getting a small policy with a rider that allows you to buy more later on.

Disability Income Insurance Policies

It is important to understand the definition of disability since policy standards differ. Ask if there are provisions for cost-of-living adjustments and guaranteed insurability options. Know both the probationary period (when the benefits kick in, usually seven to thirty days) and the waiting period (usually thirty days to one year).

Determine whether the insurance is noncancelable or guarantee renewable. Finally, understand the amount and duration of benefit; group plans tend to pay a fixed gross income percentage but most individual disability income policies pay a flat monthly benefit.

Long-Term Care

Long-term care is non-hospital medical and personal care for chronic medical conditions. Determine whether the cost of premiums outweighs the cost of a potential nursing home stay. If you have a family history of disabling diseases or if you are a male, your chances of needing long-term care increases. If you have family members who will provide care, this can reduce long-term care costs. Finally, since most assets have to be depleted before Medicaid will cover any costs, consider purchasing long-term care if you are older than sixty-five and have a net worth more than $100,000 and income more than $50,000.

Long-Term Care Policy

Check long-term care policies to determine if they include Alzheimer's disease coverage as well as at least one year of home health or nursing home coverage, including intermediate custodial care. There should be a guarantee against nonrenewal or cancellation due to age or deteriorating physical or mental health, and you should have the right to return the policy within thirty days for a refund.

Study the outline of coverage that explains the policy's benefits, limitations, and exclusions in great detail; this will also help comparison shop against other policies. Make sure there is not a requirement for policy holders to be hospitalized before they receive home healthcare or nursing home benefits, or a requirement that they have to receive a higher level of care first before they can receive lower care levels.

IMPORTANT POLICY PROVISIONS

There are some important policy provisions to think about when purchasing long-term care insurance, including the type of care. Some policies only offer nursing home care and some only offer home health care, while others also include assisted-living, adult daycare, alternative care, and community-care; respite care for the caregiver is also a possibility.

Find out if preexisting conditions are covered. Understand how much the policies will reimburse per day as well as for how long these benefits will be covered; some coverage is only for a year while others are for the insured's lifetime. Ask about the waiting period, which is usually between ninety and 100 days. Know the requirements for eligibility and what services are covered, including skilled, intermediate, and custodial care. Check to see that there is guaranteed renewability and be wary of those that have an optional renewability. Find out the premium levels and if there is inflation protection.

PURCHASING GUIDELINES

It is a good idea to buy long-term care insurance before you need it; if you are diagnosed with a serious illness, you will become uninsurable at that point. It is important to buy the coverage that you need, but not more coverage than you need. Make sure the policy has provisions for skilled, intermediate, custodial care, adult daycare centers, and assisted living facilities. If you have family caregivers or home health services, then you only need nursing home coverage. It's important to understand what the policy covers and when it pays benefits, as well as how the policy defines benefit eligibility, the amounts paid, benefit periods, and the services covered.

Investments

Savings Account

While savings accounts typically yield only around 2 percent, they are safe because they are insured. After thousands of banks failed in the Great Depression, the federal government created the Federal Deposit Insurance Corporation (FDIC) to insure money in savings accounts up to $100,000. In this way, if a credit union or bank were to go out of business, your money would still be safe. Sometimes, a low minimum balance is required to keep a savings account active without being charged a fee, but sometimes there is no minimum balance required, depending on the type of bank and account.

Interest

A bank savings account pays interest because the bank is borrowing the money from you. The bank lends your money to other people, and by charging a higher interest rate on that loan than the interest rate they are paying you, they are able to make money. Since the interest in a savings account is compounded daily and paid monthly, you can also receive interest on the money that has been earned as interest.

Two Types of Savings Accounts

The two types of savings accounts that banks offer are a basic savings account and a money market account.

- A basic savings account usually does not require a minimum balance, but it also has a very low interest rate. However, you can take money out of a basic savings account whenever you want
- A money market account pays a higher interest than a basic savings account but it also may require a higher minimum balance. Also, you can only to write a minimum number of checks (usually three) each month and you may only be able to make a certain number of withdrawals each month

Savings Program Starting Strategies

To help start a savings program, look at your spending habits to see where you can cut back. Have your employer regularly deduct money from your paycheck and automatically deposit it into your savings account. Deposit any unexpected extras like raises and bonuses in your savings account, and reinvest the interest and dividends made from your savings account.

Work a little more to earn extra money, and if any loan payments end, write checks for those same amounts but deposit them into your savings account. Keep track of the returns you receive on your savings account, and if it's only 2 or 3 percent, consider opening a money market account. Establish a retirement plan and contribute to it on a regular basis, and splurge every now and then to feel good and make saving money easier.

CDs

CDs (certificates of deposit) differ from other savings types because the money deposited has to stay put for a certain amount of time. With a CD, you deposit your money for a specified amount of time, usually anywhere from three months to a number of years; the longer the period of time, the higher the interest rate. CDs earn more interest than savings accounts and money market accounts, but there is a penalty if you take your money out before the time is up.

TREASURY BILLS

Treasury bills (T-bills) are a simple way for the government to raise money to help pay off the national debt. T-bills are popular because they are affordable (they start in denominations of $1,000), are risk-free since they are backed by the US government, and are exempt from state and local taxes.

T-bills are issued through a bidding process at auctions, and the bids can either be noncompetitive (you receive the full amount of securities you want as determined at the auction) or competitive (you specify the return that you want, but if it is too high, you may only receive a portion of the securities or none at all). The one downside to T-bills is that they are so safe that they do not yield great returns.

STOCKS

Stock is basically ownership in a company; investors participate in the profits of that company, which is what gives it its value. Stocks change in price minute to minute, and you pay a commission to buy or sell. Common stocks offer a chance to hit it big if the price skyrockets. Since common stockholders are actually owners of the company, they will receive their prorated share of the earnings and dividend income only after the company's other obligations have been met. Common stockholders need to be aware that it is possible no return on investment is a possibility.

BONDS

Bonds are publicly traded IOUs in which the bondholders lend money to the issuer of the bond. Investing in bonds is popular because they can provide a high current yield and can generate substantial gains when market interest rates fall. Bonds can be used aggressively for individuals who actively seek capital gains, and conservatively for individuals who seek high current income. Due to the high quality of bond issues, they may also be used for the long-term preservation and accumulation of capital.

BONDS AND STOCKS CONTRAST

When you buy stock, you are in essence buying ownership in the company. Bonds are a type of long-term debt; when you purchase bonds, you are a creditor of the company and that company pays you back over the life of the bond. Stocks provide higher rates of returns than bonds but they are far less stable. Additionally, bonds stabilize and diversify a portfolio. People who hold common stock have ownership or equity position whereas bondholders do not.

SINKING FUND

A sinking fund is the pool of money set aside by a business or the government to repay a bond issue over time. How the bond will be paid off is important to investors. Some bonds specify the yearly repayment schedule as well as how much principal will be retired each year. Sinking funds usually start one to five years after the issue date and continue each year thereafter until the issue is all or mostly paid off.

BOND ISSUES TYPES

A single issuer of bonds can have many bonds outstanding at a time. While bonds can be differentiated from one another due to maturities and coupons the kind of collateral behind them also distinguishes them. Bond issues are either senior or junior standing, with senior bonds being backed by a legal claim on the issuer's specific property. This claim acts as the collateral for the bonds. Senior bond issues include mortgage bonds (secured by real estate) and equipment bonds (secured by certain types of equipment and favored by airlines and railroads). Junior bonds are only backed by the issuer's promise to pay interest and principal in a timely manner; there is no collateral.

Call Feature

A call feature specifies whether a bond can be retired before its scheduled maturity date, and if it can, under what conditions. There are three main types of call features:

- free call
- noncallable
- deferred call

A freely callable bond can be retired early. A noncallable bond means the issuer cannot retire the bond before it matures. A deferred call keeps the bond from being retired until after a certain period of time passes from the date of issue, meaning the issue cannot be retired during the deferment time but becomes available for retirement thereafter.

Bond Market Segments

The four segments of the bond market are the treasury, agency, corporate, and municipal.

- Treasury bonds were created by the US Treasury to help meet the federal government's ongoing needs, have a maturity of more than ten years and pay interest twice a year
- Agency bonds are issued by divisions of the US government and usually provide higher yields than Treasury bonds
- Corporate bonds are issued by corporations, and can come in the form of industrials, public utilities, rail and transportation bonds, and financial issues
- Municipal bonds are issued by states, counties, cities, and other government divisions, and unlike other bonds, their interest income is federally tax free

Convertible Bonds

Convertible bonds are only found in the corporate market and have features of both corporate bonds and common stocks. They are issued as unsecured, but are allowed to be converted into a particular number of shares of the issuing company's stock during a certain time period.

A convertible issue has a conversion privilege that accompanies it, and this clearly states the conditions and specific nature of the conversion feature, such as exactly when the bond can be converted. The conversion ratio states the number of shares of common stock that the bond can be converted into.

Bond Rating System

Bond ratings receive letter grades for their investment quality and these ratings are widely understood and used in the corporate and municipal bond markets. Two of the best known rating agencies are Moody's and Standard & Poor's. When a new corporate or municipal issue appears on the market, professional bond analysts calculate both its default risk exposure and its investment quality. The issuing organization's financial records are looked at carefully and its future prospects assessed. This allows a bond rating to be assigned that is indicative of how quickly and efficiently the issuing organization will repay its debt. Once after a new issue is rated, it is not finished: outstanding, older bonds are reviewed regularly to make sure their assigned ratings are still valid.

Pricing of a Bond

Figuring the fair price of a bond is known as bond valuation. Theoretically, the value of a bond is calculated using the present value relationship, or the cash value it would be expected to generate.

Pricing the bond is done by determining the appropriate discount rate. Once the pricing and its relative sensitivity has been estimated, the yields and coupons can then be determined. In corporate and municipal markets, bonds are priced in decimals. Treasury and agent bond quotes are given in thirty-seconds of a point, with1 point equaling $10.

Mutual Fund

A mutual fund is an investment strategy in which money is collected from many investors and professionally managed. The fund manager trades the collected money, investing it in bonds, stocks, short-term money market accounts and other investment vehicles. Any net proceeds or losses are paid out to the investors on a yearly basis. Mutual funds are a popular investment choice for individuals because they offer a number of investment opportunities and services that are appealing to investors. Mutual funds are one of the three basic types of investment companies in the United States (the other two are unit investment trusts and closed-end funds).

Usage

Mutual funds can invest in several types of securities with the most common being cash instruments, bonds, and stock although there are a lot of other categories. Sector funds are any stock funds invested primarily in a particular industry's shares, like technology. Both stock and bond funds can invest in mainly US securities (domestic funds), US and foreign securities (global funds), or foreign securities (international funds). Bond funds differ according to their risk, issuers type (e.g., government agencies, corporations, or municipalities), or maturity of the bonds (short- or long-term).

Regulatory, Accounting, and Tax Rules

Mutual funds are subject to a special set of regulatory, accounting, and tax rules. Unlike most other types of US businesses, mutual funds are not taxed on their income as long as 90 percent of it is distributed to shareholders and the funds meet certain diversification requirements as set by the IRS. Also, the earnings from mutual funds usually do not change as it passes on to the shareholders. Mutual fund distributions are tax-free to the shareholder if they are tax-free municipal bond income. Depending on how the mutual fund earned the distributions, taxable distributions are either ordinary income or capital gains. (Net losses are not distributed or passed through to the investors of mutual funds.)

Fund Manager Role

Professional fund managers try to choose investments they think will align with the purpose of the fund's investment predict the future performance of chosen investments, oversee cash flow for mutual funds, and constantly adjust the mutual funds' investment portfolios. The fund manager is hired by a management company to administer the fund, and this company can also fire the manager. Fund managers charge a fee for their services, and this fee is a percentage of the fund's average assets during its management. A fund can be managed by one person, by two people who act as co-managers, or by a team of three or more people. When looking for a fund manager, look for someone with a history of long-term, consistent fund performance.

The Economist

The Economist is an authoritative weekly newspaper that provides anonymous (collaboratively written) opinions and analysis of business and finance. It is a good, objective financial resource to consult when investing. It covers the latest world and American stock indices as well as commodity prices, live stock prices, intraday and historical stock charts, financials for numerous companies, weekly economic and financial indicators, currency information, and rankings and ratings. A weekly economic statistics feature addresses items such as employment statistics as well as special statistical features.

The Wall Street Journal

The Wall Street Journal is a newspaper that primarily covers national and international business and financial news and issues. Sections include marketplace (which covers health, technology, media, and marketing industries), money and investing (which covers and analyzes international financial markets), economic issues, and personal investments. Its personal investments section has such regular columns as Cheapskate, The Intelligent Investor, Deals and Dealmakers, Fundtrack, Investing, Marketwatch, Tip of the Day, Starting Out, Encore, Reinvent, Ask Dow Jones, Common Sense, and Family Money, which can be quite helpful to an individual doing personal financial planning.

Retirement and Estate Planning

Retirement Planning Problems

The three biggest problems people face with retirement planning are waiting too long to start, investing too conservatively, and not putting enough into retirement. Since people in their twenties are typically not earning as much as they will in later years and may have immediate financial obstacles like student loans or childcare, they may not start saving for retirement as early as they should. Those who invest too conservatively (e.g. using savings accounts instead of other riskier but higher-yielding investment vehicles) may not accumulate enough money for retirement. Finally, those who do not put enough away may not reach their desired retirement goals.

Retirement Income Planning

When planning for retirement, it is important to identify the sources of income you expect to have. Know if you'll receive a pension from your employer, and if so, how it will be calculated. Figure out much can be expected from Social Security by checking the annual statement sent by the Social Security Administration. If you participate in a tax-deferred savings plan on your own, keep up-to-date on its current balance, and if you've set aside money for retirement in taxable accounts, keep abreast of the amounts. If you put money into a retirement savings plan sponsored by your employer, check to see how much it has accumulated and determine what the amount will be worth when you retire.

Short-Run Time Frame Strategy

Planning for retirement is difficult because unforeseen economic and personal budget changes such as job change, job loss, major medical expenses and the like cannot be anticipated. One way to plan for retirement is through a series of short-run time frames. To do this you need to state retirement income objectives as a percentage of present earnings. If, for example, you want to have a retirement income equal to 85 percent of your final take-home pay, you can calculate the amount desired to meet this need. It is a good idea to revise and update this plan every three to five years.

Long-Term Approach to Retirement Planning

A long-term approach to retirement planning lets you figure the level of income you want upon retirement, as well as the amount of funds you will need in order to meet that standard of living. Planning thirty years into the future will help calculate how much needs to be invested now. Of course, market and economic conditions are unpredictable, so it is a good idea to have alternative plans for your retirement planning goals and strategies.

Retirement Planning Tips

To get the most out of retirement planning, figure out how much money you will need to retire comfortably, taking into consideration where you will live when you retire and what the cost of living is in that area. Figure anticipated Social Security benefits and put additional money into an IRA. Know the ins and outs of your employer's pension or 401(k) plan, and if you change jobs, roll your plan over to an IRA or another tax-sheltered program instead of cashing it out.

Retirement Planning Review

It is a good idea to review a retirement plan every few years to make sure you're still on track to reach your retirement goals, and revise them if necessary. Make sure that retirement income projections and spending patterns have not changed, and see if investments are performing as expected. Consider whether your allocation of assets is still accurate. Finally, if you are not meeting your retirement goals, figure out how to contribute more to your retirement fund.

RETIREMENT INCOME SOURCES

The three main sources of income for retired people are Social Security, assets (e.g. savings, stocks, and bonds), and pension plans. Almost every retired employee is entitled to Social Security income and about half receive benefits from some type of pension. It is important to keep in mind that the amount of money earned pre-retirement as well as the length of time worked greatly impacts retirement earnings. Additionally, around 65 to 85 percent of retired workers receive some income from savings and investment assets.

SOCIAL SECURITY BENEFITS

In order to receive Social Security benefits, it is necessary to file an application with the Social Security Administration which determines eligibility for benefits. If a worker has been employed in a job that is covered by Social Security for at least forty quarters (they do not need to be consecutive) or ten years, they should be able to receive full Social Security benefits. Also, if a deceased worker has six quarters of coverage during the three years before death, the surviving spouse and dependent child also qualify for monthly benefits.

OLD AGE BENEFITS

Any fully-covered worker born before 1960 who reaches full retirement age (between sixty-five and sixty-seven) is eligible to receive lifelong old-age benefits. People born after 1960 must reach age sixty-seven for these benefits. However, since Social Security provides only a percentage of the amount the worker earned while employed and since its coverage is being paid out faster than people can pay into it, it is not a good idea to rely on Social Security alone. In certain circumstances, spouses may be able to receive an additional percentage of the retiree's amount, as well. If both the husband and wife have worked, both are eligible for Social Security benefits and can choose to take their individual shares or benefits of the higher-paid spouse.

SURVIVOR'S BENEFITS OF SOCIAL SECURITY

A spouse is entitled to receive survivor benefits from Social Security if a covered worker dies. A small lump sum is distributed immediately, followed by monthly benefits thereafter. In order to receive monthly payments, the surviving spouse has to be sixty years old or caring for dependent and unmarried child/children of the deceased. If the deceased's child/children turn sixteen before the surviving spouse reaches age sixty, the monthly benefits will stop and the spouse will not receive them again until reaching sixty.

EMPLOYEE RETIREMENT INCOME SECURITY ACT OF 1974

The Employee Retirement Income Security Act of 1974 (ERISA) is a federal law that sets minimum standards for private health, retirement, and benefit plans. Employers are not required to participate in plans, but if they do, these standards must be met. Critics of ERISA feel that participants give up Seventh Amendment rights to a jury trial and cannot sue in state court for contractual damages, wrongful death, or punitive or punishment damages. Employers may choose to avoid ERISA by shopping around for other insurance plans that are less expensive and offer more individual options tailored to their needs.

COMPANY PENSION PLANS PARTICIPATION

Pension plans are a type of benefit plan whereby employees receive a certain amount of money calculated at a fixed percentage rate upon retirement based on salary and years of employment. The employee, the employer, or both may make contributions to this plan, but only the employer takes on the investment risk. Pension plans sponsored by the employer are covered by the Pension Benefit Guarantee Corporation. Different employers require different years of service before an employee is eligible for the pension plan, and if an employee leaves his job, his pension plan stays with the employer.

Contribution Plans and Defined Benefits Plans

With a defined contribution plan, an account is set up for an individual member; the amount the employee and employer must contribute is agreed upon. The risks taken and the rewards reaped are incurred solely by the employee, not the employer. Once employees retire, they receive the monthly benefits purchased with their contributions.

Under a defined benefits plan, benefits are paid out no matter how well or poorly the retirement funds have done; if funds do not do well, it is the employer's responsibility to make up the difference so that the terms of the plan are met and the employee receives the plan's benefits. This plan only states how the benefits, not the contributions, will be calculated.

Cash Balance Plan

The cash balance plan is similar to a traditional defined benefits plan but also contains features of a defined contribution plan. Like traditional pension plans, the company alone pays for the pension, controls the investments, and guarantees payout upon retirement. It is like a defined contribution plan because a small percentage of the employee's salary is contributed. Each employee has a separate account set up for that shows how much the account has grown at any given time.

With a cash balance plan, the company guarantees that the account will earn a minimum return rate.

PBGC

The Pension Benefit Guarantee Corporation (PBGC) was created by Congress to protect workers' and retirees' retirement incomes in private sector benefit pension plans. It's privately funded from the fees that ERISA-regulated employers are charged. Eligible workers are guaranteed certain benefits from an employer even if the employer's plan does not have adequate assets. The law sets the maximum pension benefit, and this benefit changes from year to year.

Supplemental Retirement Plans

There are three basic kinds of supplemental retirement plans: profit-sharing, thrift and savings, and salary reduction plans.

- In a profit-sharing plan, employees of a company receive some of the company earnings; employees are encouraged to work harder since they will benefit if the company is financially successful.
- With a thrift and savings plan, a company contributes the same amount of money that an employee does, helping to supplement pension and other fringe benefits.
- With a 401(k), part of the employee's salary is withheld and invested. Taxes on both the contributions and account earnings are deferred until the employee withdraws the funds.

Operating Policies of a 401(k)

Employees may not know that if they leave a company too soon—usually before three years—they might not get a match. If a loan has been taken out against the 401(k) and the employee leaves the company, the employee must immediately pay back the loan or the employer will treat it like a withdrawal and charge taxes plus a 10 percent penalty. If the account has less than $5,000 the employee can cash out but will have to pay taxes plus a 10 percent penalty. Additionally, an employee who leaves the company may have to buy a tax-advantaged investment, which doesn't make sense since 401(k) plans are already tax-deferred.

Retirement Plans, Their Provisions and Benefits

When looking at retirement plans and their provisions and benefits, know what the retirement age is and penalties for early retirement. Have a clear understanding of specific options, benefits, and contributions of the plan as well as the formulas that are used to calculate them.

Understand vesting procedures, including when you are fully vested and whether the company uses a cliff procedure (employees are fully vested after a certain number of years) or graded procedure (employees are vested little by little with a gradual increase over time). It's also important to understand eligibility requirements. Find out if the plan is contributory; if so, determine how much you and the company will each contribute.

If the plan is noncontributory, determine how much of your salary the company contributes. Also, know if there are any voluntary supplemental programs and how much of your contributing salary the company will match.

Keogh Plan

A Keogh plan is for self-employed people to establish tax-deferred retirement plans for themselves and their employees. Like 401(k) plans, payments are taken as deductions from taxable income, reducing the amount of taxes self-employed individuals have to pay. Keogh accounts can be started at banks, insurance companies, brokerage firms, mutual funds, and other financial institutions.

Any income earned in Keogh accounts must be reinvested in the account, and this income will continue to grow tax-free. Contributions and earnings cannot be taken until the age of 59 ½ or upon becoming disabled or seriously ill; any early withdrawals may be penalized with a 10 percent tax.

IRAs

An IRA is not a type of investment. Rather, it is just like any other investment account that can be opened with bank, credit union, stockbroker, mutual fund, or insurance company. The only difference is that the trustee is an institution and the form clearly designates as an IRA. Anyone who is employed may open an IRA account, but the type of account (and tax status) depends on a number of things, such as income level and other retirement plans. The purpose of IRAs is to encourage retirement savings.

Types of IRAs

Roth IRAs can be opened by couples who file jointly and have adjusted gross incomes of up to $206,000 (single people may have incomes up to $124,000), as of 2020. It does not matter if they also have other retirement or pension plans. A Roth IRA is a popular choice because yearly contributions are made with after-tax dollars, and all earnings in the account grow tax-free.

A traditional (deductible) IRA can be opened by anyone who does not have a retirement plan, and income level does not matter. Also, couples who file jointly and have adjusted gross incomes of less than $124,000 (as of 2020) can also get a traditional IRA. A nondeductible (after-tax) IRA can be opened by anyone regardless of income or retirement plan at their workplace. Earnings from a nondeductible IRA accrue tax-free and will not be taxed until they are withdrawn.

Annuity

An annuity liquidates an estate in an orderly way to provide protection against economic challenges that could result should an individual outlive personal financial resources. During an accumulation period, premiums are paid toward an annuity; during the distribution period, annuity payments are made. A life insurance company will guarantee monthly payments on a regular basis under a pure life annuity contract, and the benefits include principal (the premiums paid by the person who bought the annuity), interest, and survivor benefits (funds for members of an annuity group who survive in each period thereafter).

Estate Planning

An estate is comprised of all of the property an individual owns at the time of death. This includes real estate, bank accounts, stocks and other securities, life insurance policies, and personal property such as jewelry, cars, and artwork. Estate planning helps an individual ensure that final wishes are granted and loved ones will be taken care of. Some common legal questions asked when a person dies are:

- What are the financial affairs like?
- What personal and real property does the individual own?
- Who will receive what from the estate?
- Are there minor children who need a personal guardian?
- In order to transfer property ownership, how much tax will need to be paid?
- What are the preferred funeral arrangements?

Choosing a Guardian During Estate Planning

When choosing a guardian in estate planning, there are several things to keep in mind:

- It should be a person who is able to provide a stable and nurturing home life for your children
- If the selected guardians already have children, are they prepared to take on more?
- Consider asking someone who is closer to your age versus your parents. Although they may be excellent grandparents, the burden of raising children may be too demanding
- Think twice about asking a husband and wife to be co-guardians to avoid a custody battle should the couple later divorce

Documents If You Become Incapacitated

In the event that you become incapacitated, there are four main documents you should have:

1. *Durable power of attorney*: A durable power of attorney grants the power to sell the home, and gives the holder legal authority to sign the sales contract for you
2. *Living will*: This lets your family and health care providers know your wishes for medical treatment should you become unable to communicate them directly
3. *Medical power of attorney*: This is someone you designate to make medical decisions if you are unable to communicate with your doctors
4. *Living trust*: This is used for holding and distributing assets in order to avoid probate

Trusts in Estate Planning

The main purpose behind a trust is the protection of assets from misuse by the beneficiaries. Creating a trust allows you control of asset distribution, not only during your lifetime, but after your death. Essentially, a trust is an agreement among three people:

- The grantor who contributes property to the trust
- The trustee who executes the purposes of the trust, and the beneficiary who receives the benefits of the trust in accordance with the trust agreement
- A trust should contain provisions of how the trustee should act given certain situations, for example, managing the money for a minor child

Asset Protection

Asset protection ensures that your estate benefits beneficiaries as you intended. Some assets that may be threatened and the trusts that can be created to protect them include:

- Your beneficiary cannot manage money: *a spendthrift trust*
- You want to provide for your spouse first and your children from a previous marriage second: *a marital trust*
- You want a portion of your estate to be used for your children's education and financial support until they are mature enough to manage the money themselves: *a children's trust*
- You want to provide financial support for your aging parents, and then direct who receives the remaining assets upon their death: *a support trust*
- You want life insurance payments to be spread out over time instead of a single payment: *an unfunded life insurance trust*

Living (Revocable) Trust

With a living (revocable) trust, you name yourself as the grantor, the trustee, and the current beneficiary, and then transfer assets to the trust. The terms of the trust mandate that it is to be used for your benefit during your lifetime; upon your death the living trust benefits your designated beneficiaries. Some reasons that you might want a living trust are:

- The assets held by the trust are not probate property and therefore not subject to the probate process.
- You can name a successor trustee so that in the event you become incapacitated, the successor trustee is obligated to follow your wishes.
- Since your successor trustee follows your wishes upon your death, you can direct certain funds remain in the trust for the education of your children or other purposes, with remaining funds payable to them at a certain point in the future.
- You can change the trust agreement in the event of a marriage, birth, divorce, death, or other circumstance.

Estate Taxes

Life insurance death benefits are usually not subject to income tax, but they are subject to estate tax. If you have a life insurance policy, the proceeds will be included as a part of the taxable estate so long as any the following conditions are met:

- The proceeds are paid to the estate
- The life insurance policy's designated beneficiary is legally obligated to use the proceeds to pay the obligations of the estate

- You had any incidents of ownership of the policy within three years of your death. This refers to any control of terms of the policy, including the right to modify beneficiary designation, your right to borrow against the policy, and your right to assign, change, or revoke the assignment of the policy to someone else. There are strategies that can legally remove death benefits from the taxable portion of the estate

DSST Practice Test

1. Which of the following is a financial goal?

a. Subscribing to the Wall Street Journal
b. Taking a long vacation
c. Buying a smart phone
d. Going out to dinner

2. Real property

a. is like a 1954 Thunderbird
b. is a new dishwasher
c. is easily moved
d. has a relatively long life

3. A personal balance sheet lists

a. impending expenses
b. assets minus debts owned
c. benefits from a company pension plan
d. financial performance over time

4. The Financial Modernization Act of 1999

a. was passed to reduce the long term impact of inflation on economic growth
b. reduced the role of the Federal Government in financial planning
c. was legislated to protect personal financial information held by financial institutions
d. is also known as the Gramm-Leach Act

5. Time value of money can be defined as

a. the concept that a dollar today is worth more than a dollar at some future time
b. the monetary growth amount that will be earned over a given period of time
c. monetary growth caused by compounding interest
d. a depository financial institution

6. Which of the following is a credit danger sign?

a. Getting a debit card
b. Opening checking and savings accounts
c. Using a credit card or cash advance to pay off other debts
d. Avoiding paying cash for large purchases

7. You can build a strong credit history by

a. paying off a loan very quickly
b. notifying a lender when you are unable to make a payment
c. exceeding an overdraft protection line
d. deducting the interest on a home equity credit line

8. Which of the following is a way to avoid credit problems?

a. Reduce the number of credit cards you carry
b. Accept every pre-approved card offer you receive
c. Apply for an affinity card
d. Go to www.bankrate.com

9. You can reduce your chances of being a victim of credit card fraud by

a. transferring balances to a card with a low introductory rate
b. letting a store clerk make extra copies of a sales/charge slip
c. applying for a line of credit
d. not putting your telephone number on a sales/charge slip

10. Besides charging interest on bank credit cards, banks may also charge a (an)

a. Fair Isaac & Co. fee
b. account activity summary
c. over-the-limit fee
d. Wage Earner Plan

11. Consumers need to be cautious about using overdraft protection because

a. of the Fair Credit Reporting Act
b. they do not want to make a habit of overdrawing an account
c. it will be difficult to switch credit cards
d. of capital

12. Straight bankruptcy is a legal procedure that

a. non-profit agencies provide
b. prevents credit card fraud
c. allows some people to wipe the slate clean and start fresh
d. transfers the balance from one card to another with a lower interest rate

13. Depreciation of a car is

a. the final cost of the car minus the down payment
b. variable, depending on how many miles you drive the car
c. the loss in value of the car over the ownership period
d. the operating cost of the car

14. What is one advantages of buying a used car?

a. It will not depreciate in value as quickly as a new car.
b. Used cars never require a down payment.
c. It won't cost as much to operate.
d. Used cars are more reliable now.

15. Which of the following negotiating tips is most useful when shopping for a car?

a. Shop at the beginning of the month when the sales people are not tired.
b. Don't subtract from the sticker price; start at the dealer cost.
c. Trade your old car in first.
d. Negotiate to get items you don't need.

16. When owning a home, the loan-to-value ratio is

a. the amount of mortgage interest you can deduct
b. the percentage of the value of the home that the lender agrees to loan
c. a result of having established a good credit profile
d. the monthly mortgage payment plus homeowners' association fees

17. What is Private Mortgage Insurance?

a. Extra insurance protection when your house is in a flood zone
b. An insurance policy that protects the lender if a borrower defaults
c. Insurance required when you put down 5%
d. Pre-paid interest that a lender charges at closing

18. How does a mortgage prequalification help a home buyer?

a. It correlates to the demand for mortgages
b. It lowers the maintenance fee of a cooperative apartment
c. It tells a prospective buyer the amount the lender will agree to loan
d. It helps the home increase in value

19. Lorraine and David are buying their first home. The agreed upon purchase price is $78,000, and they have enough money to put 10% down. They have been approved by their lender for a 30-year-fixed mortgage with a cost of 1.5 points. How much will the points cost them?

a. $1053
b. $1170
c. $780
d. $1500

20. What is a good piece of advice for consumers shopping for a big-ticket purchase?

a. Go to a rent-to-own outlet
b. Set aside unexpected money for future use
c. Don't buy an extended warranty on a plasma TV
d. Don't waste a lot of time; buy at the first store you visit

21. Which of the following is a red flag for the IRS?

a. You filed Form 8283 for a non cash charitable gift valued at more than $500.
b. You received Form 1099 from the bank where you kept a savings account.
c. You took a home office deduction.
d. You had a 401k contribution.

22. To qualify for a tax filing status as Head of Household you must

a. file your return separately from your spouse
b. not be married and pay more than half the upkeep on a home for you and a dependent
c. have a spouse who died within two years of the tax year
d. complete a Form W-4 designating this tax status

23. Which of the following is not considered taxable income?

a. Farm earnings
b. FICA payments
c. Alimony received
d. Annuities

24. Adjustments to gross income are which of the following?

a. Paid alimony
b. Lottery winnings
c. Capital gains
d. Medicare tax

25. An example of a tax credit is

a. itemized deductions
b. tax preparation computer software
c. portfolio earnings
d. child and dependent care expenses

26. Allowable itemized deductions include

a. some education expenses
b. limited partnership tax shelter
c. investment interest
d. dependent exemption

27. Which of the following is an amended return?

a. A return filed with Form 4868
b. Interest earned
c. A return showing a corrected dollar amount
d. A return filed with Form 1040EZ

28. When discussing insurance, risk is defined as

a. loss control
b. adverse selection
c. economic loss
d. underwriting

29. Decreasing term life insurance

a. keeps a level premium throughout all periods
b. is debt liquidation
c. is its cash value feature
d. costs more than other types of insurance

30. Which of the following is an advantage of a universal life insurance policy?

a. It is not a legal agreement.
b. It has changing protection levels.
c. Its interest is paid at the current rate of interest.
d. It has fees and charges.

31. Homeowners or property insurance does not protect against

a. acts of nature
b. theft
c. electrical fire
d. war

32. What is an important question to ask when choosing a health care plan?

a. How much income will be needed to maintain an adequate lifestyle?
b. How much money will I pay to use a doctor outside the plan's network?
c. How often is my primary doctor available?
d. What hospitals are in my area?

33. A feature of disability income insurance that is always important is

a. the probationary period
b. nursing home coverage
c. creditor protection
d. higher yield

34. When considering a long-term care insurance policy, it is important to look for

a. employer offered benefits
b. RV insurance
c. guarantee against non-renewal or cancelation due to age or health
d. disability definition

35. The difference between a CD and a money market account is

a. only a money market account is incurred by the FDIC
b. CDs are auctioned by the US Treasury on a regular basis
c. interest earned on a money market account is free from state and local income taxes
d. a CD must remain deposited for a specified period of time.

36. Which of the following is a good strategy when establishing a savings program?

a. Splurge every now and then
b. Withdraw dividends and interest when paid
c. Consider upgrading your lifestyle
d. Hold off paying bills

37. A good point about investing in bonds is

a. they provide income.
b. they have no minimum balance requirement.
c. investors can participate in profits earned.
d. their interest is equal to the difference between the price paid and value at maturity.

38. Why is a sinking fund important to investors?

a. It is a good option if you have extra money you will not need soon.
b. It specifies how a bond is going to be paid off over time.
c. It establishes a payroll deduction plan with your employer.
d. It lends money to the insurer of the fund.

39. Senior bond issues are

a. contributions to a retirement plan
b. short term debt instruments offered by the US Treasury
c. backed by a legal claim
d. the result of many banks that failed during the Great Depression

40. What is an important aspect of a convertible bond?

a. The return is free from state and local taxes.
b. They are issued as unsecured.
c. Interest income is free from federal taxes.
d. They are priced in thirty-seconds of a point.

41. The purpose of a bond rating system is to

a. determine whether a bond can be retired
b. determine if it can be secured by certain equipment
c. compare exchange rates using the Big Mac Index
d. calculate a bond's default risk exposure

42. Ivanka has just been hired as a professional fund manager for ABC Mutual Funds. Which of the following would not be one of her duties?

a. Forecast cash flow in and out of the fund
b. Withhold federal taxes from distribution on municipal bond income
c. Invest in foreign securities
d. Distribute net proceeds or losses to investors on a yearly basis

43. Which is a common mistake when planning for retirement?

a. Revising retirement goals every few years
b. Figuring out how much money will be needed to retire
c. Treating a retirement fund like a savings account
d. Starting a retirement account at age 24

44. Ethan's retirement fund is falling short of its goals. What is one thing that he can do to correct the situation?

a. Increase his contributions to his fund
b. Find out how much his pension will be
c. Take an early retirement
d. Roll his savings account into a 401(k)

45. Jeannette has a 15-year-old son. She is 59. Her husband died and she is receiving social security benefits. Which statement is true?

a. Her social security benefit will stop and then restart when she is 60.
b. Her social security benefits will go up when she is 60.
c. Her social security benefits will stop when her son turns 16.
d. Her social security benefits will continue uninterrupted.

46. What effect has the Employee Retirement Income Security Act of 1974 had on pension plans?

a. More people opened retirement accounts.
b. More companies offered pension plans.
c. Pension plans paid better than before.
d. The government offered pension plans to employees.

47. A defined benefits pension plan

a. bases benefits on the performance of the retirement fund
b. has a separate account set up by the company for each employee
c. pays benefits regardless of how the retirement funds perform
d. protects workers' and retirees' retirement incomes

48. Which describes a profit-sharing supplemental retirement plan?

a. A company contributes money equal to a proportion of the employee's contribution.
b. Company employees are able to receive some of the company earnings.
c. Part of the employee's salary is withheld and invested.
d. Workers are guaranteed certain benefits to be paid by an employer.

49. What is one provision of a Keogh plan?

a. Contributions must stay in the account until the owner turns sixty-five.
b. It can help reduce the tax bills of self-employed individuals.
c. It cannot be extended to employees.
d. Early withdrawals are not subject to a tax penalty.

50. What is the maximum income a couple can earn and still open a Roth IRA?

a. $88,000
b. $124,000
c. $196,000
d. There is no maximum income.

Answer Key and Explanations

1. B: A long vacation is a specific future financial goal; the other three choices are not. Choice A might be a good way to keep up on what is going on in the world of finance, but is not a goal. Neither are choices C or D.

2. D: Real property has a relatively long life. It also cannot be moved. Choices A and B are incorrect because they describe personal property. Choice C is incorrect also since real property cannot be moved, while personal property can be.

3. B: A balance sheet lists assets minus debt. Choice A is incorrect; it is not a list of impending expenses. Choice C has nothing to do with net worth. Choice D is also incorrect; an income and expense statement measures financial performance over time.

4. C: It was a protective measure. Choices A and B are incorrect. There is no way to reduce the impact of inflation, and there was no mention of reducing the role of government. Choice D is incorrect. It was also known as the Gramm-Leach-Biley Act.

5. A: Time value of money allows an accurate comparison of dollar values that occur at different points of time. Choice B is the future value of money. Choice C is incorrect; time value has nothing to do with an annuity or compound interest. A depository institution is basically a bank, so choice D is incorrect also.

6. C: Using credit to pay off other credit is dangerous. Choice D is one reason people apply for credit. Open checking and savings accounts helps establish credit. Debit cards are popular because they carry no high interest costs, so neither Choice A nor B is correct.

7. B: The lender may make an arrangement to help you avoid being labeled a late payer. Choice A is not correct because paying cash doesn't help build a strong credit history. Choice C, exceeding an overdraft protection line, will actually harm your credit. Choice D only refers to the fact that a home equity credit line is the only type of consumer loan that qualifies for this tax treatment.

8. A: Two cards is the most a person should have. Accepting every offer you receive may result in too much credit. Choice C, an affinity card, is merely a standard bank card that has a sponsor, such as a non-profit organization. And going to a site like bankrate.com is only a way to compare rates, making Choice D incorrect as well.

9. D: Never put personal information on any sales or charge slip. Choice A is a method of lowering monthly payments if you can pay most or all of your balance off before the rate goes up. Choice B is a sure way to invite fraud. And Choice C is the maximum amount of credit that a bank will allow.

10. C: It is a fee that is incurred if a card holder goes over the credit limit. Fair Isaac & Co. is a provider of credit scores. Choice B appears on a monthly statement and includes previous balance, new charges and finance charges. Choice D is not correct, either.

11. B: It is a bad habit and the fees are usually high. Choice A refers to credit bureau errors. Choice C comes into play when shopping for a better credit card rate. And capital is one of the Cs of Credit–the amount of unencumbered assets a borrower owns—so Choice D is incorrect.

12. C: It is a court ordered procedure that about 70% of people filing for bankruptcy choose. Non-profit agencies provide credit counseling services so choice A is not correct. Fraud and bankruptcy are two different things. And Choice D is not a legal procedure.

13. C: It is the difference in the price paid and what you could sell it for. Choice A is the amount financed. Depreciation cannot be variable, which means Choice C is incorrect. A car's operating costs are fuel, insurance, tires and maintenance charges, making choice D also incorrect.

14. D: Technological advances over the years have meant better and more reliable cars. Choice A is incorrect; the car will depreciate. Choices B and C are too generalized to be correct.

15. B: Know the cost of the car by checking out dealer costs before you go into the dealership and negotiate from that cost up. Choice A is not correct; the end of the month is best because quotas may not have been met. It is better to trade your old car after you have agreed on a price for the purchase, so choice C is wrong. Choice D is a red herring; you wouldn't want to pay for items you didn't need or want.

16. B: When the down payment is subtracted from the purchase price, the loan amount divided by the price gives a loan-to-value ratio. Choice A refers to the tax write-off benefit of home ownership. Choice C is one sign you are ready for home ownership. Homeowner association fees are only paid when you own a condominium.

17. B: Private Mortgage Insurance lowers a lender's risk when the buyer doesn't have a large down payment. It is required when you put down less than 20%. Flood insurance is required when you home is in a flood zone, so choice A is incorrect. Choice D refers to mortgage points.

18. C: The home buyer then knows what price range to look in. Choice A refers to mortgage points charged by lenders. Cooperative maintenance fees are set by a board of directors, making choice B incorrect. In Choice D, any increase or decrease in a home's value is determined by the market and demand.

19. A: $70,200 is the mortgage amount x 1.5%.

20. B: Applying a bonus or a tax refund means you will finance less. A rent-to-own choice will probably cost the most, so choice A is wrong. Choice C is reversed. It can be a good idea to buy an extended warranty on an item that has a high probability of needing repairs. You should always visit several stores as prices vary, making choice D also incorrect.

21. C: The IRS looks at returns with home office deductions closely because there are many ways to misinterpret the regulation. You must include Form 8283 if the non cash gift is more than $500, so choice A is incorrect. You will always receive a Form 1099 for interest you earned on a savings account and Retirement (401k) offer tax advantages but are not considered a red flag, so neither Choice B nor D is correct.

22. B: This filing status is intended to help single parents with dependent children. Choice A describes married filing separately taxpayers, so it is incorrect. If your spouse died within two years, you would file as a qualifying widow or widower, so this one is incorrect also. And form W-4 is completed when one starts employment to determine the amount of federal income taxes withheld.

23. B: This isn't income. It is payroll taxes deducted for Social Security and Medicare. Choice A is income and taxable, as are Choices C and D, so those are both incorrect, also.

24. A: Paid alimony is deducted from your gross income. Lottery winnings are added to gross income, so choice B is incorrect. Any capital gain is taxable income and Medicare tax is part of the taxes withheld, making Choices C and D incorrect as well.

25. D: Child care expenses are a tax credit that reduce taxes owed instead of taxable income. Itemized deductions are subtracted from gross income, so choice A is incorrect, as is Choice B. Software is used by many to prepare their own taxes, but does not constitute a tax credit. Choice C is incorrect as well. Portfolio earnings are income and taxable.

26. C: Investment interest and residential mortgage interest are allowable deductions. Education expenses and exemptions are adjustments to gross income, not allowable itemized deductions, so choice A and D are incorrect. Choice B is a form of taxable income.

27. C: Form 4868 is used to receive an extension of time to file, so choice A is incorrect. Choice B is not correct either. Interest earned is a form of taxable income. Form 1040EZ is a simpler return form you can use if you meet certain requirements, so choice D is also wrong.

28. C: When you have a financial interest-health, home, car or business, and that item is lost or its value reduced, there is a risk of financial loss. Choice A is an activity that reduces the severity of loss when it happens. Adverse selection occurs when high risk clients apply for and receive insurance coverage, so choice B is incorrect as well. Underwriting is the process insurance companies use to decide who they will insure and the rate they will charge, making choice D incorrect.

29. A: Decreasing term life insurance is an option because death rates increase each year a person is alive. And while the premium remains the same, the amount of insurance decreases. Choice B is incorrect; Debt liquidation is one of the components used in assessing a family's total economic needs when using the need analysis method for estimating how much life insurance is needed. The cash value feature applies to whole life insurance, which provides s small return or investment, so choice C is incorrect. And decreasing life insurance offers lower initial premiums than other types of insurance, so choice D is not correct.

30. C: Universal life insurance combines death benefits with a tax-sheltered savings/investment account that pays interest. Choice A is not correct. All types of insurance policies are legal agreements. And both Choices B and C, changing protection levels and fees and charges are disadvantages of a universal life insurance policy, so they are incorrect as well.

31. D: War is a peril that cannot be reasonably insured. An act of nature, like a home struck by lightning, is covered, as is loss due to theft or vandalism, which means Choices A and B are not correct. Choice C is not correct either. Every accidental fire is covered.

32. B: Health care plans vary considerably as to cost when going outside the network. Choice A is a question to ask when figuring out how much life insurance you should have. Choice C could be asked, but it isn't central to what health care plan you might choose, but to what primary doctor you would choose. Choice D should be a consideration when choosing where to live, not which health plan to choose.

33. A: The time delay is from the date the policy is issued until benefits can begin and can be from 7 to 30 days. Nursing home coverage is included in long-term care insurance, so choice B is incorrect. Choice C, creditor protection, is a feature of life insurance and is not the right choice. Choice D is also not correct.

34. C: It is important to have coverage if a physical or mental condition gets worse. Choice A and D are aspects of disability life insurance protection. Choice C is also incorrect since RV insurance is a form of transportation insurance.

35. D: A CD (Certificate of Deposit) must remain deposited for a specific period. There is a penalty if you withdraw money early. Generally, the longer the CD, the higher the interest rate. Choice A is incorrect; all types of savings accounts are insured. If your bank were to go out of business, your money is protected. Treasury bills, or T-bills, are auctioned by the US Treasury Department, not CDs, so choice B is incorrect. Choice C is incorrect as well. Only Treasury bills that are auctioned are free from local and state taxes.

36. A: Splurging on occasion feels good and makes saving easier. Choice B is incorrect; you should reinvest interest and dividends so the account will grow more quickly. Choices C and D are wrong as well. You should keep your lifestyle as it is and deposit any bonuses in your savings. If you are having a hard time paying bills, review your spending habits to see where you can cut back.

37. A: Bonds provide income from the interest payment received over the life of the issue. Choice B applies to a basic, or passbook, savings account. Choice C refers to stock ownership. Choice D is how T-bills pay interest, so it is incorrect as well.

38. B: A sinking fund specifies the yearly repayment schedule for the issue. Choice A is correct for a certificate of deposit (CD). And Choice C is one strategy to get a savings program started. Choice D provides a definition of bonds–publicly traded IOUs in which bond holders lend money to the issuer of the bond.

39. C: Senior bonds are backed by a legal claim on the issuer's specific property, which acts as collateral for the bonds. Choice A is a strategy to get a savings program stared. Choice B refers to US T-bills, and Choice D is about the FDIC which was created by the federal government in 1933 after thousands of banks failed.

40. B: Convertible bonds are only found in the corporate market and have a provision that during a specified time they can be converted into shares of stock. Choice A refers to T-bills. Choice C refers to municipal bonds, so they are both incorrect. Treasury and agency bonds are priced in thirty-seconds of a point, so choice D is also incorrect.

41. D: Corporate and municipal bonds are rated on investment quality and these ratings are reviewed regularly to make sure they are still valid. All the other choices are incorrect.

42. B: Interest income from municipal bonds is not federally taxable. Choice A and D are both straightforward activities of a mutual fund manager. And many mutual funds do specialize in investments in foreign (international) funds, making choice C incorrect.

43. C: If you treat your retirement fund like a savings account your funds won't grow very rapidly. Choice A is not correct. This is something that people should do, as is Choice B. It is never too young to start a retirement account, so choice D is incorrect also.

44. A: This will directly increase the amount in Ethan's retirement fund. Finding out how much his pension will be is a good idea, but that won't rectify the problem of falling short of goals, so choice B is incorrect; Taking an early retirement won't affect his retirement fund nor will rolling over his saving account into a 401(k), so both C and D are incorrect as well.

45. D: Since she will be turning 60 at the same time her son turns 16, her benefits will continue without interruption. Choice A is incorrect since her benefits will not stop. Choice B is not correct either. She will continue to receive the same amount. Choice C is incorrect since she will be 60 when he is 16.

46. A: The Act motivated people to establish retirement accounts. Choice B is incorrect since the opposite was true. Pension plans did not pay more or less because of the Act. Government already offered pension plans to employees when this Act was passed.

47. C: This option pays benefits despite how well or poorly the retirement funds perform, with the company contributing when necessary. Choice A is what a defined contribution pension plan does. Choice B describes the cash balance plan and Choice D describes the Pension Benefit Guarantee Corporation (PBGC), so they are also not correct.

48. B: This is the definition of a profit-sharing supplemental retirement plan. Choice A is the definition of a thrift and savings plan while Choice C describes a salary reduction plan or 401(k) plan, so neither is correct. Choice D describes the Pension Benefit Guarantee Corporation (PBGC).

49. B: Choice A is incorrect since the age is fifty-nine-and-a-half. Choice C is not true and early withdrawals may be subject to a 10 percent penalty, so choice D is incorrect as well.

50. C: $196,000 is the maximum income for a couple in 2020 to make a full Roth IRA contribution; the maximum for a single person is $124,000. Choice D applies to a nondeductible (after-tax) IRA.

How to Overcome Test Anxiety

Just the thought of taking a test is enough to make most people a little nervous. A test is an important event that can have a long-term impact on your future, so it's important to take it seriously and it's natural to feel anxious about performing well. But just because anxiety is normal, that doesn't mean that it's helpful in test taking, or that you should simply accept it as part of your life. Anxiety can have a variety of effects. These effects can be mild, like making you feel slightly nervous, or severe, like blocking your ability to focus or remember even a simple detail.

If you experience test anxiety—whether severe or mild—it's important to know how to beat it. To discover this, first you need to understand what causes test anxiety.

Causes of Test Anxiety

While we often think of anxiety as an uncontrollable emotional state, it can actually be caused by simple, practical things. One of the most common causes of test anxiety is that a person does not feel adequately prepared for their test. This feeling can be the result of many different issues such as poor study habits or lack of organization, but the most common culprit is time management. Starting to study too late, failing to organize your study time to cover all of the material, or being distracted while you study will mean that you're not well prepared for the test. This may lead to cramming the night before, which will cause you to be physically and mentally exhausted for the test. Poor time management also contributes to feelings of stress, fear, and hopelessness as you realize you are not well prepared but don't know what to do about it.

Other times, test anxiety is not related to your preparation for the test but comes from unresolved fear. This may be a past failure on a test, or poor performance on tests in general. It may come from comparing yourself to others who seem to be performing better or from the stress of living up to expectations. Anxiety may be driven by fears of the future—how failure on this test would affect your educational and career goals. These fears are often completely irrational, but they can still negatively impact your test performance.

Elements of Test Anxiety

As mentioned earlier, test anxiety is considered to be an emotional state, but it has physical and mental components as well. Sometimes you may not even realize that you are suffering from test anxiety until you notice the physical symptoms. These can include trembling hands, rapid heartbeat, sweating, nausea, and tense muscles. Extreme anxiety may lead to fainting or vomiting. Obviously, any of these symptoms can have a negative impact on testing. It is important to recognize them as soon as they begin to occur so that you can address the problem before it damages your performance.

The mental components of test anxiety include trouble focusing and inability to remember learned information. During a test, your mind is on high alert, which can help you recall information and stay focused for an extended period of time. However, anxiety interferes with your mind's natural processes, causing you to blank out, even on the questions you know well. The strain of testing during anxiety makes it difficult to stay focused, especially on a test that may take several hours. Extreme anxiety can take a huge mental toll, making it difficult not only to recall test information but even to understand the test questions or pull your thoughts together.

Effects of Test Anxiety

Test anxiety is like a disease—if left untreated, it will get progressively worse. Anxiety leads to poor performance, and this reinforces the feelings of fear and failure, which in turn lead to poor performances on subsequent tests. It can grow from a mild nervousness to a crippling condition. If allowed to progress, test anxiety can have a big impact on your schooling, and consequently on your future.

Test anxiety can spread to other parts of your life. Anxiety on tests can become anxiety in any stressful situation, and blanking on a test can turn into panicking in a job situation. But fortunately, you don't have to let anxiety rule your testing and determine your grades. There are a number of relatively simple steps you can take to move past anxiety and function normally on a test and in the rest of life.

Physical Steps for Beating Test Anxiety

While test anxiety is a serious problem, the good news is that it can be overcome. It doesn't have to control your ability to think and remember information. While it may take time, you can begin taking steps today to beat anxiety.

Just as your first hint that you may be struggling with anxiety comes from the physical symptoms, the first step to treating it is also physical. Rest is crucial for having a clear, strong mind. If you are tired, it is much easier to give in to anxiety. But if you establish good sleep habits, your body and mind will be ready to perform optimally, without the strain of exhaustion. Additionally, sleeping well helps you to retain information better, so you're more likely to recall the answers when you see the test questions.

Getting good sleep means more than going to bed on time. It's important to allow your brain time to relax. Take study breaks from time to time so it doesn't get overworked, and don't study right before bed. Take time to rest your mind before trying to rest your body, or you may find it difficult to fall asleep.

Along with sleep, other aspects of physical health are important in preparing for a test. Good nutrition is vital for good brain function. Sugary foods and drinks may give a burst of energy but this burst is followed by a crash, both physically and emotionally. Instead, fuel your body with protein and vitamin-rich foods.

Also, drink plenty of water. Dehydration can lead to headaches and exhaustion, especially if your brain is already under stress from the rigors of the test. Particularly if your test is a long one, drink water during the breaks. And if possible, take an energy-boosting snack to eat between sections.

Along with sleep and diet, a third important part of physical health is exercise. Maintaining a steady workout schedule is helpful, but even taking 5-minute study breaks to walk can help get your blood pumping faster and clear your head. Exercise also releases endorphins, which contribute to a positive feeling and can help combat test anxiety.

When you nurture your physical health, you are also contributing to your mental health. If your body is healthy, your mind is much more likely to be healthy as well. So take time to rest, nourish your body with healthy food and water, and get moving as much as possible. Taking these physical steps will make you stronger and more able to take the mental steps necessary to overcome test anxiety.

Mental Steps for Beating Test Anxiety

Working on the mental side of test anxiety can be more challenging, but as with the physical side, there are clear steps you can take to overcome it. As mentioned earlier, test anxiety often stems from lack of preparation, so the obvious solution is to prepare for the test. Effective studying may be the most important weapon you have for beating test anxiety, but you can and should employ several other mental tools to combat fear.

First, boost your confidence by reminding yourself of past success—tests or projects that you aced. If you're putting as much effort into preparing for this test as you did for those, there's no reason you should expect to fail here. Work hard to prepare; then trust your preparation.

Second, surround yourself with encouraging people. It can be helpful to find a study group, but be sure that the people you're around will encourage a positive attitude. If you spend time with others who are anxious or cynical, this will only contribute to your own anxiety. Look for others who are motivated to study hard from a desire to succeed, not from a fear of failure.

Third, reward yourself. A test is physically and mentally tiring, even without anxiety, and it can be helpful to have something to look forward to. Plan an activity following the test, regardless of the outcome, such as going to a movie or getting ice cream.

When you are taking the test, if you find yourself beginning to feel anxious, remind yourself that you know the material. Visualize successfully completing the test. Then take a few deep, relaxing breaths and return to it. Work through the questions carefully but with confidence, knowing that you are capable of succeeding.

Developing a healthy mental approach to test taking will also aid in other areas of life. Test anxiety affects more than just the actual test—it can be damaging to your mental health and even contribute to depression. It's important to beat test anxiety before it becomes a problem for more than testing.

Study Strategy

Being prepared for the test is necessary to combat anxiety, but what does being prepared look like? You may study for hours on end and still not feel prepared. What you need is a strategy for test prep. The next few pages outline our recommended steps to help you plan out and conquer the challenge of preparation.

Step 1: Scope Out the Test

Learn everything you can about the format (multiple choice, essay, etc.) and what will be on the test. Gather any study materials, course outlines, or sample exams that may be available. Not only will this help you to prepare, but knowing what to expect can help to alleviate test anxiety.

Step 2: Map Out the Material

Look through the textbook or study guide and make note of how many chapters or sections it has. Then divide these over the time you have. For example, if a book has 15 chapters and you have five days to study, you need to cover three chapters each day. Even better, if you have the time, leave an extra day at the end for overall review after you have gone through the material in depth.

If time is limited, you may need to prioritize the material. Look through it and make note of which sections you think you already have a good grasp on, and which need review. While you are studying, skim quickly through the familiar sections and take more time on the challenging parts.

Write out your plan so you don't get lost as you go. Having a written plan also helps you feel more in control of the study, so anxiety is less likely to arise from feeling overwhelmed at the amount to cover.

Step 3: Gather Your Tools

Decide what study method works best for you. Do you prefer to highlight in the book as you study and then go back over the highlighted portions? Or do you type out notes of the important information? Or is it helpful to make flashcards that you can carry with you? Assemble the pens, index cards, highlighters, post-it notes, and any other materials you may need so you won't be distracted by getting up to find things while you study.

If you're having a hard time retaining the information or organizing your notes, experiment with different methods. For example, try color-coding by subject with colored pens, highlighters, or post-it notes. If you learn better by hearing, try recording yourself reading your notes so you can listen while in the car, working out, or simply sitting at your desk. Ask a friend to quiz you from your flashcards, or try teaching someone the material to solidify it in your mind.

Step 4: Create Your Environment

It's important to avoid distractions while you study. This includes both the obvious distractions like visitors and the subtle distractions like an uncomfortable chair (or a too-comfortable couch that makes you want to fall asleep). Set up the best study environment possible: good lighting and a comfortable work area. If background music helps you focus, you may want to turn it on, but otherwise keep the room quiet. If you are using a computer to take notes, be sure you don't have any other windows open, especially applications like social media, games, or anything else that could distract you. Silence your phone and turn off notifications. Be sure to keep water close by so you stay hydrated while you study (but avoid unhealthy drinks and snacks).

Also, take into account the best time of day to study. Are you freshest first thing in the morning? Try to set aside some time then to work through the material. Is your mind clearer in the afternoon or evening? Schedule your study session then. Another method is to study at the same time of day that you will take the test, so that your brain gets used to working on the material at that time and will be ready to focus at test time.

Step 5: Study!

Once you have done all the study preparation, it's time to settle into the actual studying. Sit down, take a few moments to settle your mind so you can focus, and begin to follow your study plan. Don't give in to distractions or let yourself procrastinate. This is your time to prepare so you'll be ready to fearlessly approach the test. Make the most of the time and stay focused.

Of course, you don't want to burn out. If you study too long you may find that you're not retaining the information very well. Take regular study breaks. For example, taking five minutes out of every hour to walk briskly, breathing deeply and swinging your arms, can help your mind stay fresh.

As you get to the end of each chapter or section, it's a good idea to do a quick review. Remind yourself of what you learned and work on any difficult parts. When you feel that you've mastered the material, move on to the next part. At the end of your study session, briefly skim through your notes again.

But while review is helpful, cramming last minute is NOT. If at all possible, work ahead so that you won't need to fit all your study into the last day. Cramming overloads your brain with more information than it can process and retain, and your tired mind may struggle to recall even previously learned information when it is overwhelmed with last-minute study. Also, the urgent nature of cramming and the stress placed on your brain contribute to anxiety. You'll be more likely to go to the test feeling unprepared and having trouble thinking clearly.

So don't cram, and don't stay up late before the test, even just to review your notes at a leisurely pace. Your brain needs rest more than it needs to go over the information again. In fact, plan to finish your studies by noon or early afternoon the day before the test. Give your brain the rest of the day to relax or focus on other things, and get a good night's sleep. Then you will be fresh for the test and better able to recall what you've studied.

Step 6: Take a Practice Test

Many courses offer sample tests, either online or in the study materials. This is an excellent resource to check whether you have mastered the material, as well as to prepare for the test format and environment.

Check the test format ahead of time: the number of questions, the type (multiple choice, free response, etc.), and the time limit. Then create a plan for working through them. For example, if you have 30 minutes to take a 60-question test, your limit is 30 seconds per question. Spend less time on the questions you know well so that you can take more time on the difficult ones.

If you have time to take several practice tests, take the first one open book, with no time limit. Work through the questions at your own pace and make sure you fully understand them. Gradually work up to taking a test under test conditions: sit at a desk with all study materials put away and set a timer. Pace yourself to make sure you finish the test with time to spare and go back to check your answers if you have time.

After each test, check your answers. On the questions you missed, be sure you understand why you missed them. Did you misread the question (tests can use tricky wording)? Did you forget the information? Or was it something you hadn't learned? Go back and study any shaky areas that the practice tests reveal.

Taking these tests not only helps with your grade, but also aids in combating test anxiety. If you're already used to the test conditions, you're less likely to worry about it, and working through tests until you're scoring well gives you a confidence boost. Go through the practice tests until you feel comfortable, and then you can go into the test knowing that you're ready for it.

Test Tips

On test day, you should be confident, knowing that you've prepared well and are ready to answer the questions. But aside from preparation, there are several test day strategies you can employ to maximize your performance.

First, as stated before, get a good night's sleep the night before the test (and for several nights before that, if possible). Go into the test with a fresh, alert mind rather than staying up late to study.

Try not to change too much about your normal routine on the day of the test. It's important to eat a nutritious breakfast, but if you normally don't eat breakfast at all, consider eating just a protein bar. If you're a coffee drinker, go ahead and have your normal coffee. Just make sure you time it so that the caffeine doesn't wear off right in the middle of your test. Avoid sugary beverages, and drink enough water to stay hydrated but not so much that you need a restroom break 10 minutes into the test. If your test isn't first thing in the morning, consider going for a walk or doing a light workout before the test to get your blood flowing.

Allow yourself enough time to get ready, and leave for the test with plenty of time to spare so you won't have the anxiety of scrambling to arrive in time. Another reason to be early is to select a good seat. It's helpful to sit away from doors and windows, which can be distracting. Find a good seat, get out your supplies, and settle your mind before the test begins.

When the test begins, start by going over the instructions carefully, even if you already know what to expect. Make sure you avoid any careless mistakes by following the directions.

Then begin working through the questions, pacing yourself as you've practiced. If you're not sure on an answer, don't spend too much time on it, and don't let it shake your confidence. Either skip it and come back later, or eliminate as many wrong answers as possible and guess among the remaining ones. Don't dwell on these questions as you continue—put them out of your mind and focus on what lies ahead.

Be sure to read all of the answer choices, even if you're sure the first one is the right answer. Sometimes you'll find a better one if you keep reading. But don't second-guess yourself if you do immediately know the answer. Your gut instinct is usually right. Don't let test anxiety rob you of the information you know.

If you have time at the end of the test (and if the test format allows), go back and review your answers. Be cautious about changing any, since your first instinct tends to be correct, but make sure you didn't misread any of the questions or accidentally mark the wrong answer choice. Look over any you skipped and make an educated guess.

At the end, leave the test feeling confident. You've done your best, so don't waste time worrying about your performance or wishing you could change anything. Instead, celebrate the successful completion of this test. And finally, use this test to learn how to deal with anxiety even better next time.

Review Video: Test Anxiety
Visit mometrix.com/academy and enter code: 100340

Important Qualification

Not all anxiety is created equal. If your test anxiety is causing major issues in your life beyond the classroom or testing center, or if you are experiencing troubling physical symptoms related to your anxiety, it may be a sign of a serious physiological or psychological condition. If this sounds like your situation, we strongly encourage you to seek professional help.

Thank You

We at Mometrix would like to extend our heartfelt thanks to you, our friend and patron, for allowing us to play a part in your journey. It is a privilege to serve people from all walks of life who are unified in their commitment to building the best future they can for themselves.

The preparation you devote to these important testing milestones may be the most valuable educational opportunity you have for making a real difference in your life. We encourage you to put your heart into it—that feeling of succeeding, overcoming, and yes, conquering will be well worth the hours you've invested.

We want to hear your story, your struggles and your successes, and if you see any opportunities for us to improve our materials so we can help others even more effectively in the future, please share that with us as well. **The team at Mometrix would be absolutely thrilled to hear from you!** So please, send us an email (support@mometrix.com) and let's stay in touch.

If you'd like some additional help, check out these other resources we offer for your exam:
http://MometrixFlashcards.com/DSST

Online Resources

Due to our efforts to try to keep this book to a manageable length, we've created a link that will give you access to all of your online resources:

mometrix.com/resources719/dsstpersonfin

It's Your Moment, Let's Celebrate It!

Share your story @mometrixtestpreparation